HOW TO BECOME A CELEBRITY LEADER IN HOSPITALITY INDUSTRY

ANUTOSH BHAKTA

All Present & Future Leaders

**PEOPLE DON'T CARE HOW MUCH YOU KNOW
THEY ONLY KNOW HOW MUCH YOU CARE**

Contents

Anutosh Bhakta is a distinguished and highly respected figure in the world of hospitality education and corporate training, with over 40 years of experience. His journey began at the prestigious Institute of Hotel Management, Kolkata, under the Ministry of Tourism, Government of India, where he completed his undergraduate studies. He then pursued postgraduate training in teacher education at the Institute of Hotel Management, Mumbai, and later earned a Master's degree in Tourism Management.

A certified trainer recognized by SAITHRDP and HCIMA, Mr. Bhakta further honed his expertise through professional training in Hotel Facility Planning, Design, and Hotel Engineering at Cornell University, New York. His education at Cornell also included specialized training in Hotel Management, Operations, Staffing, Budgeting, and Control.

As a National Trainer and Consultant for Training Need Analysis, recognized by the Department of Personnel and Training, Government of India, Mr. Bhakta has made significant contributions to hospitality training across the nation. He has completed advanced courses in Training Design and Direct Trainer Skills, in collaboration with Thames Valley University, UK.

Mr. Bhakta's career has been a blend of operational excellence and educational leadership. After transitioning from hospitality operations to education in the early 1980s, he served as the Divisional Head of the Hotel Management division at the Indian Institute of Business Management. He later joined the Institute of Hotel Management,

Kolkata, where he served for over 20 years, before taking on the role of General Manager, Learning and Development, with the Jaypee Group of Hotels. In this capacity, he also served as the Principal of their Centre of Excellence.

From early 90s, Mr. Bhakta balanced his responsibilities as a professor with his role as a hospitality trainer at a renowned star hotels, dedicating his weekends to this pursuit. Since 2011, he has focused full-time on corporate training, working closely with various star hotel groups and other corporations. It was during this period that he identified a critical gap in leadership development—why some qualified and experienced individuals struggle to lead effectively.

Drawing from his extensive experience, Mr. Bhakta developed a simple yet powerful set of guidelines designed to help anyone build a loyal following among their team members and beyond. His insights provide a clear path to becoming a successful leader—a "Celebrity Leader"—in the hospitality industry.

It is a great pleasure to introduce this essential guide by Mr. Anutosh Bhakta, a respected figure in hospitality management and a professor who has significantly influenced my career and the careers of many others. The book, "How to Become a Celebrity Leader in the Hospitality Industry," offers more than just advice; it is a comprehensive guide to leadership, reflecting Mr. Bhakta's extensive experience and insights.

The hospitality industry is unique, requiring both technical skills and strong interpersonal abilities. Throughout my career, the lessons I've learned from Mr. Bhakta have been invaluable. He emphasizes the importance of "human engineering"—the skill of understanding, motivating, and leading people, which is the foundation of effective leadership. This concept is thoroughly explored in his book.

Mr. Bhakta's method is both practical and insightful. He divides the journey to becoming a respected leader into two main parts: first, building a strong foundation in leadership through the right mindset, skills, and tools; and second, applying the 4C concepts—Connection, Communication, Conversion, and Community—to create a committed and motivated team.

This book is a valuable resource for both current hotel managers and those aspiring to leadership roles in hospitality. It not only guides you on how to succeed in the industry but also shows how to do so with joy and fulfilment. The ultimate goal is to create a work environment where team members are excited to come to work, driven by a shared purpose and respect for their leader.

Mr. Bhakta's insights into the human side of leadership are particularly impactful. He reminds us that, unlike machines, people are influenced by their emotions and mental state. By mastering "human engineering," leaders can foster a positive and productive workplace where employees excel both personally and professionally.

I encourage you to read this book with an open mind and a willingness to transform your approach to leadership. Whether you are an experienced professional or just starting in hospitality management, the lessons in this book will provide you with the tools to become a celebrity leader—one who not only succeeds but also inspires others to succeed.

Ambar Mazumdar
Chief Executive Officer
Chanalai Group of Hotels and Resorts
Phuket
Thailand
www.chanalai.com
Alumni of IHM, Kolkata

"Experience is what you get when you don't get what you want" – Anutosh Bhakta, circa summer of May 1998. Walking in to a classroom filled with 'crew cut' young boys and 'hair-oiled' young girls little did we know that life would be anything akin to being Celebrity Leader(s) in Hospitality Industry let alone survive the de-glamour of being part of a Basic Training Kitchen and eating the now greatly missed SDH (Student Dining Hall) DBC (Dal Bhaat Curry) for three years at the Institute of Hotel Management, Catering Technology & Applied Nutrition nestled in an industrial area of Calcutta (now Kolkata), West Bengal, India.

There Mr. Bhakta was – standing out amongst all the rest of the faculty in his two tone well ironed suit. Representing the epitome of hoteliers that he was entrusted to create. I have known Mr. Anutosh Bhakta (Sir) as we fondly refer to him for over 25 years, having first met him on Day 1 of my tryst with being an hotelier. Never one to not give you a head to toe quick scan and read through your thoughts, Anutosh Bhakta Sir has always been a magician mentor and one who assesses the human capital gap to goal within minutes of interacting with you.

No mincing words with roses although he comes from a Front (of the house) office background, Anutosh always spotted the dot (aka dark spot) in the personality and volunteered to work on it, provided we were attitudinally up for it. Largely most of us benefited and thus have survived the rigor of the industry.

How to become celebrity leader in Hospitality Industry – represents the wisdom collated through the over 40 years that Anutosh Bhakta

Sir has been in the industry and is a brilliant read. Today, the façade of Human Engineering is represented by the count of Leaders each of us have been able to create and this book would definitely be a perfect referral in upping the game. Each chapter of the book has been carefully sequenced and if followed would surely increase the leaders fan base and thus enhance objectivity of the team. In particular the chapter on Common Sense – Your hidden sixth sense to wisdom would appeal to the reader's the most as truly Hoteliering is no Rocket science but application of Common Science and that is science of the Human Touch.

Mastering the Art of People Management is something that Anutosh – The Author highlights perfectly as he himself has always broken it down to the 'T' Manage-men-T (manage men tactfully). A very basic of the vital importance of a strong root is covered beautifully in this masterpiece. Reference to the 10 Cardinal rules that every leader should be conscious about are like the 10 commandments that leaders should follow enroute their journey to becoming successful.

A must have collection and a must read for all hoteliers – for all of us can become Celebrity Leaders.

Prashant Chadha
General Manager
Marriott Ahmedabad

Preface

During my 40 years stint in hospitality education as Educator and hospitality trainer I have noticed that there are students who are not very successful in the industry. Out of which I've also noticed that there are students who are very good in academics throughout their course, even then they fail to move forward in the industry. Don't take me wrong, I'm not saying that those who are good in academics they are failures in the industry. At the same time, I have seen there are students who are not that good in academics but they are absolutely successful in the industry and moved forward very fast and became successful leaders.

Initially I was really surprised that why it is so? Though the academic input is same for all students.

I could understand, there must be some gap between the input in the college and the output result in the industry. I had a strong feeling that the students must not have acquired certain skills in the college which are absolutely required to be successful as a leader in the industry but in the initial few years I did not have any answer for that.

In the early 90s I took up the extra assignments on the weekends to train hospitality industry professionals in some renowned star hotels Along with my regular assignment as professor in the hospitality college. I have also noticed that all managers are not good in their role though they are having required degrees and experience. Whereas, some are having basic skills & knowledge and comparatively having less experience BUT they are successful in their role and they are liked

& accepted by everybody in spite of not having required degrees and sufficient experience.

Again, I was surprised.

From 2011, I was completely involved in conducting a training workshop on a full-time basis in different renowned hospitality organizations and I got the opportunity to observe all level managers whether it is a lower level, middle level or a top-level manager how they function and what impact they create among the team members.

Here also I found the same pattern which tells, in spite of having required degrees and sufficient experience in the industry many of them are not at all successful to manage their team members for positive outputs.

After so many years, I could realize the missing link why all are not successful in spite of having required knowledge & experience but some are successful.

In one word, the missing link is the CONNECTION and to be very precise heart to heart connection with the team members from the leader.

That is the reason, I developed a simple concept of 4Cs to build a strong connection with the team members because I understood that human beings are not machines so they cannot be only process driven rather there should be more psychology driven. The performance of any human being both qualitative as well as quantitative depends on their state of mind. So, a good leader or a successful leader should understand human engineering very well besides their knowledge and skill because that is the main catalyst to produce the finest result in the industry. It is very simple

because a leader cannot work alone he has to get the work done through people that is why managing people psychologically is utmost important.

These observations, motivated me to write this book so that the present managers in the hospitality industry who are aspiring to become a successful celebrity leader gets the benefit.

I also strongly feel that hospitality management students should also get the hang of this concept, so as soon as they join the industry they're ready to start their journey as a leader Without any trial and error method.

In this book I have discussed this 4Cs (Connection-Communication-Conversion-Community) concept Step by step and in detail which I'm sure will help the present and future leaders of the hospitality industry to become absolutely successful and can make them a celebrity leader in the Industry.

I would like to give my sincere thanks to all my hospitality education students who had given me the opportunity to teach them and also to all managers of all corporate houses in the industry who had also given me the opportunity to train them.

Last but not the least I would like to thank my wife for helping me to organize the writing dedicatedly every day without fail. Without her motivation it was not possible for me to complete this book. Thank you so much for being my wife.

Introduction

My heartfelt gratitude to you for purchasing this book. Probably you have been attracted with the title of the book How to Become a Celebrity Leader in Hospitality Industry. Believe me this is not a clickbait title. Yes you can be a celebrity leader very easily in the industry provided you follow a very very simple technique of human engineering. During my stint of 40 years in the industry I have seen many leaders who have very good skill in their domain and very good knowledge but even then they turned out to be a very bad leader. I have observed they are deficient in one skill that is they don't have the knowledge or the skill of Human Engineering.

At the same time I have also seen people having average skill in their domain but they are extremely successful as a leader in the industry because they have the most important skill that is human engineering. They understand how to handle people in the workplace and get the work done by them easily while keeping them happy.

Why I am saying that human engineering is the most most important skill to become a successful leader and to become a popular leader. The reason is the leader cannot do every work himself. He has to get the work done through people and the most important thing is this the output both qualitative as well as the quantitative of human beings depends on the state of their mind. Human machines. are not beings.

Let me give you one example: suppose if you have a 20-watt LED lamp and whenever you switch on that light, it will give the same amount of light. Correct?

But we human beings on an average work for 9 hours in a day but you must agree with me that's our output both qualitative as well as quantitative is not same everyday where as we get the same remuneration every day.

So, what is the difference between a machine and the human being in terms of their output both qualitative as well as quantitative?

It is very simple; the performance of human beings depends on their state of mind.

When they feel good they tend to perform better and when they feel bad their performance falls down drastically.

Now, it is the responsibility of the leader to make their subordinates feel good at their workplace, so that they are extremely happy to do their job and produce qualitative as well as quantitative output. This is the main job of a leader and if a leader is prudent in doing so, he can very easily get the work done by his subordinate as per the company's goal and standard.

In this book, I will reveal how you can master this skill step by step . So that your subordinate and your colleagues will feel good to work with you and definitely you will agree with me when we work from our within we all produce better performance at ease.

When they feel comfortable and at peace at the workplace and glad to work with you, they become your fan.

And when they become your fan they will love your association and in no time they will start seeing you as a celebrity leader because they will love your association.

In the next chapter I will discuss how to become a celebrity leader and how to increase your fan followers in your organisation & beyond.

How you should make your professional root strong, so that the foundation of your leadership skill is strong enough to lead your subordinates at ease and to get the best possible output from them.

No one enters this world as a great leader or an extraordinary individual straight out of the maternity ward. Greatness is not something we are born with, but rather something we cultivate over time. Every single person, regardless of where they start in life, holds within them the potential to achieve greatness. However, realizing this potential requires more than just recognizing it—it demands action. To lead a truly remarkable life, we must tap into this innate potential and make conscious efforts to develop it.

The journey to greatness involves making the right decisions, particularly in our careers, where our choices can either propel us toward our full potential or hold us back. It is through these thoughtful choices, combined with hard work, perseverance, and continuous learning, that we can unlock our true capabilities and shape the life we desire.

Make Your Leadership Root Strong for Ever Lasting Impact

In this chapter we will discuss how we can make our professional roots strong enough so that we can influence people very easily to get the work done both qualitatively and quantitatively by always keeping them happy.

Before we start, let me give you an example, A car has many parts like engine, steering, gears, wheels etc, but to run the car efficiently the most important part is the engine, right?

Similarly, we human beings have many parts to function for example our brain and our body parts. To function flawlessly the most important part is our brain that is our mind.

So, let me discuss in short about the importance of our mind to get the qualitative and the quantitative output.

We have 2 kinds of mind that we all know.

1. Subconscious mind
2. Conscious mind

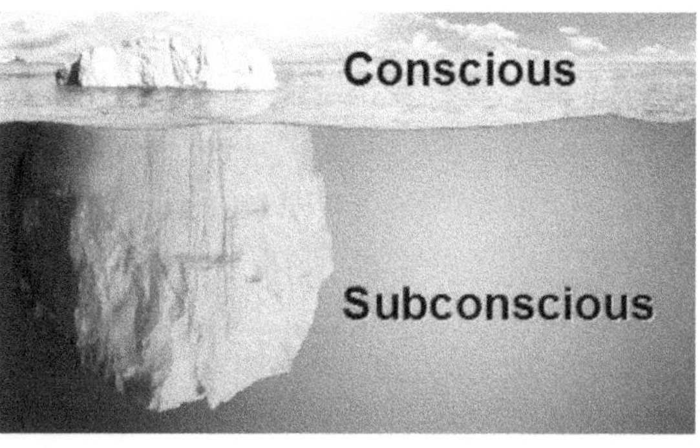

The research shows the contribution of the subconscious mind is more than 86% to get the result and contribution of the conscious mind is approximately 14%.

Let us understand what is subconscious mind and what is a conscious mind.

Let me explain this with the help of an example, we all use the mobile phone alright?

Now in the mobile phone we install lot of apps which function from inside at the same time we have the mobile screen where we can see the output.

Now here the apps are nothing but the software which is being programmed inside the mobile and depending on the software we get the output which we can see or experience on to the screen.

For example, Facebook is an app which is being programmed and installed in the mobile and when we use this Facebook we can see the result on the screen according to the programming done in the Facebook app.

Similarly, we have the app for songs and music, Say Amazon Music. So, this is a software which has been installed and programmed in a particular manner inside the mobile app and when we use this, we can have the output on to the screen through our sound system in the mobile.

So, we can say the apps are the software and the screen are the hardware. The way the software is being programmed the hardware will act accordingly.

Similarly, our subconscious mind is the place where we program many things for our activities.

It is something like that, in the subconscious mind there are many kinds of approved programming that is the apps which are being installed but the difference is, in the mobile or in the computer there are pre-installed apps which are being programmed by the manufacturer and sometimes we also can install our own app but in the subconscious mind all apps for our activities has to be programmed by us. The way we program our apps in the subconscious mind we will be getting the result accordingly.

So now we can understand that how subconscious mind is so important for all of us to have our desired activities in life. If the subconscious mind is programmed in a negative manner then we will be getting negative results. Similarly, if it is being programmed in a positive manner will be getting the positive result always.

That is why to take care of subconscious mind for the success in life, be it a leadership, be it relationship, be it our health, everything is being controlled by our subconscious mind.

So, it is very clear that to get the best result we need to work on our subconscious mind on a regular basis so that we get the best possible result in our life in every domain.

Now the question is how we can strengthen our professional root stronger so that we can have the total control in our profession and we can build up our leadership quality very easily so that people will love to work with us happily and they become our fan with no time and they will love to work with us, they will love to follow our directives and they will love to grow with us. This is how within a very short period of time you can be a celebrity leader in your domain.

In the next chapter will discuss how we can strengthen our root and what we should focus on.

We need to focus on 3 things to become a successful celebrity leader.

1. Mind set

2. Skills set

3. Tool set

Let us discuss in detail of all above three, In the next chapter.

Shine Bright: Three Focus Points for Leading Like a Star

Three Focus Point to Become Celebrity Leader

In the last chapter I have mentioned 3 important things which we need to focus on to develop ourselves as a successful leader.

So, we need to focus on 3 things

1. Our Mindset
2. Our Skill set
3. And our Tool set

In this chapter we will discuss all these three in detail.

Mindset

Now to strengthen our mindset which is most important for our success, first we need to rewire our subconscious mind which I explained in the previous chapter that how important is the subconscious mind for us.

For rewiring our subconscious mind, the foremost thing, we need to do is to instill our positive belief system.

Let me explain what a belief system is and how it helps us to grow and to get success in any field of our life.

The Power of Belief: Shaping Your Journey

The beliefs you hold at the outset of a journey shape the entire path you will follow. Transforming yourself requires first transforming your belief system. A bus conductor becomes a superstar because, even while conducting, he believed he was meant for something greater.

A tea seller rises to become a prime minister because he didn't see himself confined to that role. An employee becomes a world-renowned entrepreneur because he realized early on that he didn't belong in his current league.

Take sports as another example. When someone is learning chess, it's their belief in their potential to be a champion that drives them forward. Not everyone who believes they will become a champion succeeds, but without that belief, success is impossible.

Positive thinking alone doesn't guarantee success, but negative thinking ensures failure.

The primary reason for poverty is the belief in one's mind that they can only remain poor. Similarly, middle-class families often stay where they are because they believe that is their destined position in life.

When your beliefs don't expand, your life doesn't expand.

Many people, despite their capabilities, aspire only to be employees in foreign lands. They achieve that but remain employees because their beliefs don't stretch beyond that aspiration.

On the other hand, some people believe they can be leaders and entrepreneurs anywhere in the world. They go on to establish organizations because their expanded beliefs manifest in their actions.

Life provides according to the size of your belief.

If you carry a spoon, the rain will fill the spoon. If you carry a bucket, it will fill the bucket. If you build a pond, the rain will fill the pond. Similarly, life will not give you more than what you believe is possible. If you believe you can only be a dancer, you will just be another dancer.

But if you believe you can transform and revolutionize the art form, you will do so.

If you think you are just meant to wear a uniform and be another face in the crowd, you will be just that.

However, if you see the uniform as a step towards leadership and creating significant change, you will open up endless possibilities.

Sitting with the belief that change is impossible means even God has given up on you. But if you believe in transformation, even the smallest thing can inspire and change you. No program is needed.

Humans are powerful magnets. As the Vedas, Quran, and Bible all suggest, we are created with a divine essence, a cosmic magnetic field. This makes us powerful bio magnetic fields, attracting or repelling opportunities based on the quality of our beliefs.

We draw towards us what aligns with our beliefs. Whether a saint approaches you or mosquitoes swarm you depends on the quality of your inner state.

Clean water attracts saints, dirty water attracts mosquitoes. The magnet within us, powered by our beliefs, determines what we attract.

Conclusion

In essence, your beliefs are the foundation of your journey. They define what you attract and what you repel. To change your life, start by changing your beliefs. Believe in greater possibilities, and your life will expand to meet those beliefs.

Now let us explore little bit about the scientific aspect of these belief system. This is also known as **Placebo Effects.**

Dr.Bruce Lipton is a renowned cell biologist, author, and speaker. He is best known for his ground-breaking research on epigenetics and the mind-body connection. He said, A gene is a blueprint.

Are you reading the blueprint or are you not reading the blueprint? And the gene does not make that decision. And what do you think controls the signal? Perception. Every cell has about 1.4 volts, not too much. 50 trillion cells in the body multiplied by 1.4 volts is 70 trillion volt of electricity in your body right now. But your mind is the government for the 50 trillion cells.

So if you change your thoughts and your mind, you can change biology. And the mind is the primary cause of illness on our planet today. So you are not the victims of your genes, because you can change any of your genes anytime. If you change your perception, you change the reading of your genes. If someone tells you you're going to have a disease and you believe that, then you can create the disease.

Perception can rewrite the genetic code. Perception controls life. No two people see the world in the same way. They have different perceptions. And sometimes your perceptions can be right, and sometimes your perceptions can be wrong. Since perception controls biology, and since they can be right or wrong, then it's more accurate to say that belief controls biology. What you believe creates your life on the inside and on the outside.

You're not a victim of your genetics. You are responsible for what unfolds in your life. The placebo effect is when you have a very positive thought that something can heal you, even if it's a sugar pill, but you believe it's the real medicine, then you can heal yourself with that. So the pill did not heal you. It was the thought that healed you. There is negative thinking, and it's called the nocebo effect.

And in the same power that positive thinking can heal you, negative thinking can kill you. So if we were growing up and programmed with stronger beliefs, we would be more powerful than we are now.

Let me give you some very powerful guidelines to strengthen and rewire your subconscious mind in a positive mode.

1. Visualization – it means on a daily basis visualise your progress in your career and how successfully you are managing your team in the coming years. Visualization is a very very powerful to make your subconscious mind believe that you are actually successful. With the help of a time machine go to the future and actually visualize after one year, 5 years, after 10 years what is your position and how you are successful. It means do not visualize in terms of future tense but visualise in terms of present tense.

2. Affirmation-take it as an everyday morning ritual. Sit in a quiet place alone and say loudly what you want to be, for example

   a. I am a successful hospitality leader

   b. I help my team members to grow into their career

   c. I am very popular among my team members

   d. My team members always produce qualitative and quantitative results on time

   e. I always satisfy my customers

   f. My customers are always happy with our service

   You can add many other things as per your need.

   This will again help your subconscious mind to believe that you are already successful and subconscious mind will start acting accordingly.

3. Daily gratitude writing – Thank your associates your colleagues your seniors your subordinates your parents your teachers your society on a daily basis. This will help you to become humble and it will be easy for you to find the quality among your associates rather than criticising them always. This will definitely help to maintain a better relation with everybody. For example

a. Thank you my parent for making me capable to work in my organization

b. Thank you my teacher for teaching me the wisdom and the skill to become successful in my life.

c. Thank you my boss for guiding me to solve the problems and helping me to grow.

d. Thank you my team members for producing desired result for the organization

e. Thank you God forgiving me the sound health to enjoy the life

You can add many other things as required.

4. Goal writing-right a short term goal and a long term goal short term goal I mean to say may be a goal for the next one month and the long term goal maybe for next one year or maybe more than that according to your need.

Find out the 4 important actions to be taken to meet the short term goal and to take these actions write down the task required to be completed against each action.

Preferably you make a goal card very I'll be writing the short term and long term goal and make sure that every day you read your goal card this will be a reminder to your subconscious mind to take action and when he will be taking actions automatically it will be getting the result so writing goal is very very important don't just keep your goal into your memory don't depend on your memory write it down and read on a daily basis and take actions accordingly this will help you to manage your team members in a more effective manner and to grow in your career at a fast pace.

At last I will suggest you if you want to reach your goal successfully and on a faster pace please listen on a daily basis "Strangest Secret by Earl

Nightingale". It will create magic in your life. Let me give you the link for this.

https://youtu.be/s0vOqcDyBoY?si=dOF3i55ECmTjhWXE

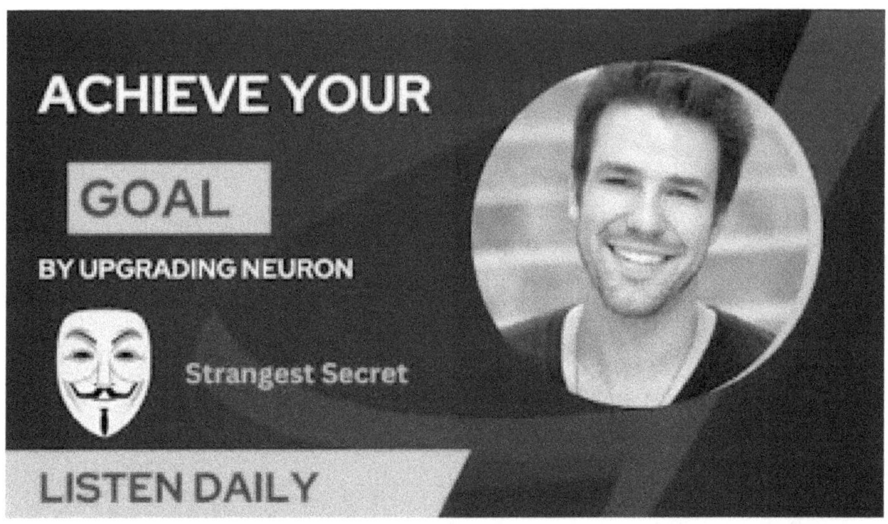

Skill Set

The next important aspect to become a successful leader is strengthen our skill set according to our field of work.

What I mean by the skill set?

It means according to our profession for example if we are in the hospitality industry and we are working in hotels the basic skills of food production, food and beverage service, front office and housekeeping And other relevant skills (as the case may be) has to be strong because you need to guide your subordinates very often for the growth of their career then only we will be able to make them feel that if I work with this person, I will grow in my career fast and they will start trusting you. Because trust is one of the most important factors when dealing with your people. So never stop learning. It is not necessary to know everything but we all can learn continuously. So, have a positive attitude to learn new things which probably we don't know yet this will help you to have a better control over your subordinates.

Tool Set

The 3rd aspect we need to focus on is our tool set. What is tool set?

In this modern age, to carry out our day to day function that is our operations we need to use many tools. Days have gone when we used to depend on the register and the files only now this is the age of computer and A I. So we need to use the tools which are suitable for our day to day function and please make sure that you as a leader must understand these tools may not be in details very details but at least you should have the knowledge that how it functions and what kind of output these different tools gives in your operations so that you have a better control over the functions and over your team members.

You will always find in the market new tools will be introduced, make sure that you learn the basics of all these tools for the reason I told in the in the above paragraph.

To be a successful leader it is more important to bring stability to our mind than our ability. We focus so much on our ability that we forget to bring stability to our mind.

4

Common Sense: Your Hidden Sixth Sense to Wisdom

In the previous chapter we have discussed in details to make our professional root strong, we need to focus on 3 things

1. Mindset
2. Skill set
3. Tool set

We have also learned that what is the importance of mindset. Because when our mind becomes strong especially by rewiring our subconscious mind we become successful as a leader and as a human being.

In this state, we don't need to chase people to get the work done both qualitative and quantitative rather we will be able to attract them very easily so that they willingly produce desired result both qualitative and quantitative.

Don't Chase People

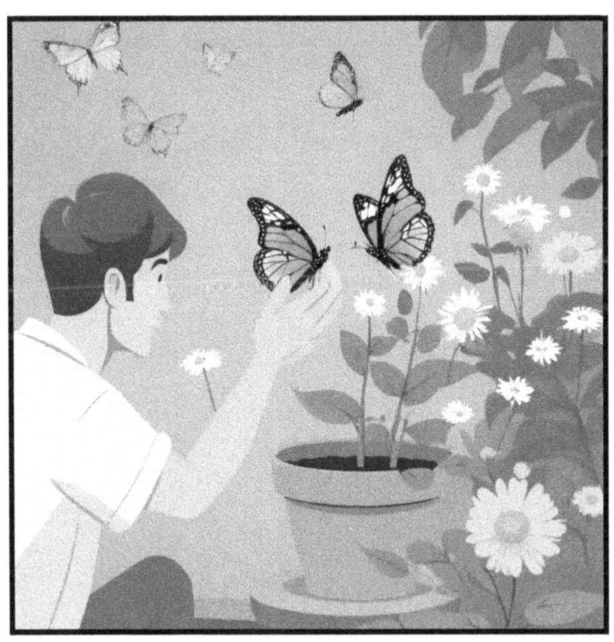

Attract People

This will make you most successful & popular leader. Soon you will increase your fan followers. People will love & enjoy your association.

Your team members will not feel that I will have to go to work rather they will love to go to work.

Your mindset will change your team members mindset.

It is said that the successful leaders they don't do the different things But they do things differently.

In the following chapters we will discuss how to do things differently so that we become absolutely successful and popular among our team members.

This will help us to attract people towards us rather than chasing people for results.

Whatever we will be discussing in the following chapters

1. Many points we know and practice.
2. Many points we know but we do not practice.
3. Many points we don't know but still we practice.
4. Many points we do not know and we do not practice.

We all know that in our industry we maintain sops that are standard operating procedures. But in my 40 years stint in the industry as well as in training I have seen that many a time sops do not work. Many a time we need to use our common sense depending on the situation we face, where sops do not give the desired result.

Common sense is very very important for all successful leaders.

Knowledge and skill without common sense has very little meaning. Common sense is our 6th sense and abundance of common sense is wisdom.

Now the question is what is common sense?

According to me **common sense is a sense which is not common to common people**

But we leaders are not common people, we are extraordinary people thus we need common sense.

Let me tell you a story which I read somewhere.

There was a renowned biscuit manufacturing company, suddenly They started getting complaints from their retailers that few cartoons they received were empty. This is a matter of their reputation, so immediately the top management took it very seriously and ordered an investigating committee to find it out what the problem was.

After investigation the committee found that in their automation section something went wrong and that is the reason their automatic packaging was not synchronizing properly, as a result during the packaging few cartoons were not filled with the biscuits.

Top management immediately contacted the machine manufacturer and asked them to rectify the fault but they came to know that it will take at least 7 days to rectify it. So they ordered that during these 7 days they will deploy more staff near the conveyor belt to check manually whether all cartoons are filled with biscuits or not.

This created a delayed operation and they could not complete the required number of packaging on time.

There was an old employee working as a labor and he suggested to the supervisor that Sir why not we put a pedestrian fan against the conveyor belt and the empty cartoon will blow away automatically and it will save our time instead of checking each and every cartoon whether it is filled with biscuits or not. This is known as common sense. This activity will never be written in the SOP.

Another example from a well-known story which is self-explanatory

There was a man named John. He could hardly complete his schooling due to some family reason. He had the desire to support his son in education to the highest level. He worked very hard and invested in his son's education. The day has come when his son became Doctorate in Astronomy.

John was extremely happy. Both of them went for a vacation in a hill station to celebrate the joy.

First night, after dinner they went to sleep in a private tent. At midnight, John saw something strange & pushed his son to wake him up.

The son woke up and said father what happened? Father said see what happened.

Son reacted WOW, so many stars in the sky. You know that star is called Vega, the brightest star in the constellation Lyra and is one of the most luminous stars in the night sky.

See that one on your right that is known as Polaris – Commonly known as the North Star, Polaris is located in the constellation Ursa Minor and is famous for its nearly fixed position in the sky.

This is how he started explaining all visible stars in the sky to his father.

After hearing for five minutes, John put a tight slap on his son's face & said stupid can't you realize that our tent has been stolen? How are we going to spend our night in this chilly weather?

You should have locked it from inside.

Now the son realized and said oh yes, it will be really challenging for us, I should have locked it before sleeping.

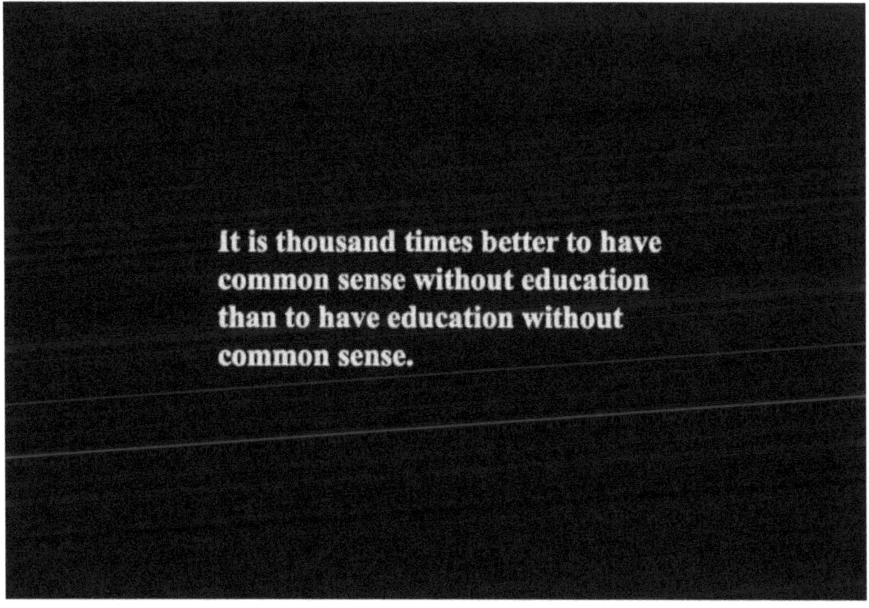

So, use your common sense whenever it is required in your daily routine activities. Don't be rigid always to follow your SOP.

5

Master Stress: Your Guide to Calm and Control

In my 40 years a stint, I have seen that most leaders face the prime challenges to overcome stress.

If you remember in the previous chapter, I discussed how important is our subconscious mind and if we can rewire our subconscious mind in a positive mode we can make our mental roots absolutely strong, so that we can handle any situation whichever comes in our way.

In this chapter let us discuss an absolute positive and effective way to combat stress in our workplace as well as in our life.

This will change our perspective about the stress in life and will be able to handle any kind of stress very effectively.

Let us understand what is stress.

Stress, in simple terms is like a fire more precisely, embers, permanent embers.

We can either control them to be harmless embers and enjoy their glow, or fan them into huge fires.

Not knowing better, many leaders do the later.

Let me give you a very simple concept and if you understand this and start believing this concept from the core of your mind I mean to say if you can make a permanent impression in your subconscious mind about this concept it will be very easy for you to handle any kind of a stress in your life and minify your worries.

Ask yourself, do you have a problem in life, you can have 2 answers one is yes and another is no. If your answer is no then why worry?

If your answer is yes, then ask can you do something about it? Again, there would be 2 answers either yes or no.

If your answer is yes then why worry. Take actions accordingly to solve the problems because it is in your hand.

If the answer is no then it is obvious that you do not have any solution in your hand, it is an external factor. So why worry which is not in your hands.

When the situation is not under your control then there is no other option but to trust your almighty, who will probably help you to come out from the problem.

Let me tell you an interesting story.

In an Airbus, there were approximately 300 passengers and during the flight in the midair the Airbus encountered a fall into an air pocket. So, there was tremendous turbulence in the aircraft and all passengers were really worried what will happen to them. Someone was screaming, few were praying to God, few went in trauma out of fear. So, it was a total chaos in the aircraft.

Somehow the pilot could take out the aircraft from the air pocket and the aircraft were stable but the aircraft faced little technical problem and due to that aircraft had to land in the nearby airport on an emergency basis.

There was an elderly person in the aircraft and next to him a 13-year-old girl was sitting. The person noticed throughout that everybody was worried and tensed whereas that 13-year-old girl was reading a book quietly and she was absolutely calm. Even after landing, she was very calm and cool.

That elderly person was really astonished that, how it is possible for that little girl to be so calm during this kind of a situation where all other passengers were almost In trauma.

That elderly person asked that little girl, my child can I ask you a question? She replied Yes uncle.

When we all were facing the turbulence everybody was stressed and worried about the situation but I have noticed you are so calm and quiet. How was it possible?

The little girl replied, uncle I do not have the control over the aircraft, it is only in the hand of a pilot.

And you know the pilot of this plane is my father. I trust my father completely and I know that he will definitely take me out of this difficult situation Then, why should I worry?

Similarly, our father, our almighty is sitting above and will definitely save us from any difficult situation.

We need to trust our father, our almighty completely, because situation is not in our control.

If you understand this concept and believe it from the core of your heart, you will be able to live peaceful life and stress-free life at the same time you will be able to produce desired result in your workplace as well as in your life.

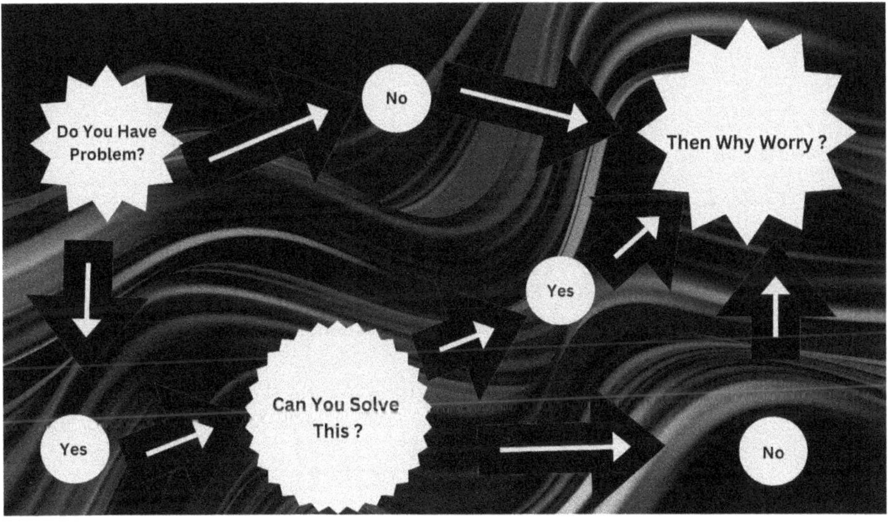

Please remember

Stress leads to Anxiety
Anxiety leads to Fear
Fear leads to Failure

6

One Man Can Make the Difference

I have seen many managers in the hospitality industry during my 40 years stint and they very often say that I have worked in a renowned organization and I was absolutely successful but you know here in this organization people are very lazy and they don't have the proper skill and knowledge. I am really surprised that how HR department is working here and how they are recruiting these kinds of people.

I really work very hard to set things right. You know, before my joining the department was worst in performance. After I joined, I really worked hard to set things right but what can I do alone? because my team members are not very skillful and knowledgeable so it is not possible to produce the result alone but still I'm working very hard day and night and because of me the department is somehow running otherwise it would have been collapsed long back.

If you are already working, I am sure that you must have heard this kind of dialogues from many managers.

If you are still a student in the hospitality management course I'm sure that you will be experiencing this kind of managers in many organizations.

You know, this kind of leaders rather, they are not leaders, according to me they are the managers and not leaders because all managers cannot be leaders but all leaders can be good managers.

I call this kind of managers as **Bhusha Managers**. In English Bhusha means Dust Ink.

Wherever they go they put black ugly impression on others.

They are always confused. They are always in a hurry. They talk very fast which is hardly understandable. Very often they speak incomplete sentences. They always believe in a fire fighting and they do not believe in planning, they do not understand the priority.

Whereas, I call a true leader/ manager as **Mango Tree Managers.**

They always give cool shadow to their team members so that they are always comfortable in their workplace.

These Mango Tree Managers are always calm, have clear concepts, and know how to delegate.

They know when to say no, they pay extra time with their team whenever it is necessary. They always protect their team members and help them to grow.

But history teaches us that "One Man Can Make The Difference".

To name a few

1. Netaji Subhash Chandra Bose
2. BR Ambedkar
3. A .P.J. Abdul Kalam
4. Vallabhai Patel
5. Mother Teresa
6. J.R.D. Tata

And in present days

1. Ratan Tata
2. N. R. Narayana Murthy
3. Nakul Anand
4. Patu Keswani

5. Jyoti Narang

6. KB Kachru

These are the few names which I have mentioned but there are so many in the industry few are very known and I have seen there are many who are not known so much but they are the excellent leaders and they can make the difference into their organizational performance.

One Man Can Make a Difference in the Hospitality Industry.

The hospitality industry thrives on providing exceptional service and memorable experiences to guests. In this context, the adage "one man can make a difference" holds significant weight. A single individual's actions can transform a guest's experience, influence the workplace environment, and even impact the success of an entire establishment.

I still remember my first organisation, where I joined as Management Trainee, there was an Operation Manager & his name was Mr. Bobby Patra. I have experienced that regular guests used to call that hotel as Bobby's Hotel instead of the original name of the hotel.

Let's explore how one person can make a remarkable difference in the hospitality industry, with real-life examples to illustrate these points.

Exceptional Customer Service

One shining example of an individual making a difference is the story of Chris, a concierge at a luxury hotel. Chris's attention to detail and genuine care for guests turned ordinary stays into extraordinary experiences. On one occasion, a family visiting for a wedding realized they had left behind an essential item. Chris not only arranged for it to be sent overnight but also provided a complimentary dinner to ease their stress. This act of kindness didn't just solve a problem; it created loyal guests who returned to the hotel annually, praising Chris's exceptional service.

Positive Workplace Influence

 HOW TO BECOME A CELEBRITY LEADER IN HOSPITALITY INDUSTRY

In addition to enhancing guest experiences, a single employee's positive attitude can uplift the entire workplace. Take Maria, a housekeeper at a resort, for example. Maria always greeted her colleagues with a smile and offered help whenever needed, regardless of her workload. Her enthusiasm was contagious, improving team morale and cooperation. This positive atmosphere led to better service overall, as employees were more motivated and engaged. Maria's attitude demonstrated that one person's positivity could ripple through the entire team, creating a more pleasant and productive work environment.

Innovation and Improvement

Innovative thinking is another area where one individual can make a significant impact. Consider the case of Ahmed, a chef at a bustling urban restaurant. Ahmed noticed that many guests requested healthier meal options. He took the initiative to develop a new menu featuring organic, locally-sourced ingredients. This change not only catered to guest preferences but also attracted a new clientele interested in healthy eating. The restaurant's popularity soared, and profits increased. Ahmed's innovative approach showed that one person's vision could lead to substantial business growth and success.

Leading by Example

Leadership is another critical aspect where one person can make a difference. Emily, a front office manager, exemplifies this. She led by example, always arriving on time, dressing professionally, and handling guest complaints with grace and efficiency. Her team observed and mirrored her behaviour, resulting in a more professional and courteous front office staff. Emily's leadership improved the hotel's reputation for excellent service, proving that one person's standards can elevate the entire team's performance.

Leadership plays a crucial role in shaping the culture and success of any organization, especially in the hospitality industry. "Leading by example" is a powerful concept where leaders influence their teams through their actions rather than just words. Extraordinary leaders who embody this principle can inspire, motivate, and elevate their teams to deliver outstanding service. Let's explore the importance of leading by example with examples of prominent leaders from the Indian hospitality industry to illustrate its impact.

Setting High Standards

One of the most significant ways a leader can make a difference is by setting high standards. Consider the example of Capt. C.P. Krishnan Nair, the founder of The Leela Palaces, Hotels and Resorts, known for his meticulous attention to detail and passion for excellence, Capt. Nair ensured that every Leela property offered unmatched luxury and service. His insistence on high standards in every aspect of hotel operation. From cleanliness to customer service, became a hallmark of the Leela brand. His team, inspired by his dedication, consistently delivered exceptional experiences to guests, establishing The Leela as one of India's leading luxury hotel chains.

Handling Challenges with Grace

Leaders who handle challenges with grace and composure set a powerful example for their teams. Arne Sorenson, the former CEO of Marriott International, is a prime example from the hospitality industry. During his leadership, Marriott faced significant challenges, including the acquisition of Starwood Hotels and the global impact of the COVID-19 pandemic. Arne's calm and compassionate leadership was instrumental in navigating these turbulent times. He approached the Starwood acquisition with a strategic vision, ensuring a smooth integration of the two companies despite the complexities involved. Later, during the pandemic, Arne communicated transparently with employees and stakeholders, making difficult decisions with empathy and a long-term perspective. His ability to lead with grace under immense pressure inspired confidence within his team and demonstrated the importance of composure, empathy, and resilience in overcoming industry-wide challenges.

Indra Nooyi, the former CEO of PepsiCo, exemplifies this leadership quality. During her tenure, PepsiCo faced significant challenges, including shifting consumer preferences toward healthier products and intense competition in the global market. Indra's calm and visionary approach enabled the company to navigate these challenges successfully. She spearheaded a strategic shift towards healthier products, balancing short-term pressures with long-term growth. Her ability to stay composed under pressure and drive transformative change inspired her team to remain resilient and committed. Indra's leadership through adversity highlighted the critical importance of grace, strategic thinking, and determination when facing challenges.

Demonstrating Commitment

Extraordinary leaders show their commitment to their work and team, fostering loyalty and dedication. Patu Keswani, the Chairman and Managing Director of Lemon Tree Hotels, exemplifies this trait. Known for his hands-on approach, Patu often visits his hotels, interacts with staff, and ensures everything is running smoothly. His commitment to inclusivity and hiring practices, focusing on providing opportunities for people with disabilities, has set a benchmark in the industry. Patu's dedication to both operational excellence and social responsibility has inspired his team to work with the same level of commitment and passion.

Encouraging Continuous Improvement

Leaders who advocate for continuous improvement inspire their teams to seek excellence. Deep Kalra, the founder of MakeMyTrip, India's leading online travel company, is an excellent example. Deep encourages his team to embrace innovation and continuous learning. Under his leadership, MakeMyTrip has consistently adapted to new technologies and changing market dynamics, maintaining its leadership position in the travel industry. Deep's focus on continuous improvement and professional development for his team has fostered a culture of innovation and excellence within the company.

Fostering a Positive Work Environment

Creating a positive work environment is another critical aspect of leading by example. Priya Paul, the Chairperson of Apeejay Surrendra Park Hotels, is known for her emphasis on creating a supportive and inclusive workplace. She promotes a culture of openness, creativity, and employee empowerment. Priya's initiatives, such as encouraging artistic expressions and fostering a collaborative work environment, have resulted in high employee satisfaction and retention. Her positive attitude and commitment to employee well-being have created a motivated and dedicated workforce that consistently delivers exceptional guest experiences.

Leading by example is a cornerstone of effective leadership in the Indian hospitality industry. Extraordinary leaders like Capt. C.P. Krishnan Nair, Arne Sorenson, Patu Keswani, Deep Kalra, and Priya Paul illustrate how their actions can inspire and elevate their teams. By setting high standards, handling challenges gracefully, demonstrating commitment, encouraging continuous improvement, and fostering a positive work environment, these leaders create a culture of excellence. Their influence extends beyond their immediate actions, shaping the entire team's behaviour and contributing to the overall success and reputation of their establishments.

In the hospitality industry, where every detail count, the actions of one person can significantly impact guests, colleagues, and the business as a whole. Whether through exceptional service, positive influence, innovative ideas, or exemplary leadership, individuals like Chris, Maria, Ahmed, and Emily show that one man—or woman—can indeed make a difference. Their stories remind us that in hospitality, where the human touch is paramount, every individual has the power to contribute meaningfully to the success and warmth of the industry.

Please remember " You Can Make the Difference" and step forward to become "A Celebrity Leader"

Craft Your Identity: The Power of Personal Branding

Personal Branding and Its Importance in the Workplace

Personal branding is about creating a unique and consistent image of yourself. It's how you present yourself to the world, both online and offline. For leaders, personal branding is crucial because it shapes how they are perceived by their teams, colleagues, and the wider industry. A strong personal brand can lead to career success, influence, and the ability to inspire others.

Why Personal Branding Matters

1. **Trust and Credibility:** A strong personal brand builds trust and credibility. When people know what you stand for, they are more likely to trust and respect you.

2. **Visibility and Recognition:** Effective personal branding increases your visibility and helps you stand out in your field. It makes it easier for others to recognize your achievements and skills.

3. **Networking Opportunities:** A well-established personal brand attracts opportunities for networking. People are more likely to connect with you if they see you as a valuable and influential person.

4. **Career Advancement:** Leaders with strong personal brands are often considered for promotions and leadership roles. Their reputation for excellence precedes them, making it easier to advance in their careers.

A great example of personal branding in the Indian context is Shah Rukh Khan, one of Bollywood's most successful actors. Shah Rukh Khan, also known as SRK, has built a strong personal brand that goes beyond his acting career.

1. **Consistency and Versatility:** SRK is known for his versatility in playing diverse roles, from romantic leads to complex characters. His consistent performances have made him a trusted name in the film industry.

2. **Public Engagement and Charisma:** Shah Rukh Khan actively engages with his fans through social media, interviews, and public appearances. His charisma and ability to connect with people have strengthened his personal brand, making him a beloved figure not just in India but worldwide.

3. **Entrepreneurial Ventures:** Beyond acting, SRK has ventured into production with his company Red Chillies Entertainment and owns the Kolkata Knight Riders cricket team in the Indian Premier League. These successful ventures have showcased his business acumen and expanded his brand into new arenas.

4. **Philanthropy and Social Responsibility:** Shah Rukh Khan is also known for his philanthropic efforts. He supports various causes, including child health and education, which has added a dimension of social responsibility to his personal brand.

By building a strong personal brand, Shah Rukh Khan has achieved unparalleled success and influence. His example shows how personal branding can play a vital role in establishing oneself as a leader not only in the workplace but also in broader social and business contexts.

How to Build Your Personal Brand

1. **Identify Your Strengths:** Understand what you are good at and what you are passionate about. These will be the core of your personal brand.

2. **Be Consistent:** Consistency is key. Make sure your actions, words, and online presence align with the image you want to project.

3. **Network and Engage:** Connect with others in your industry. Attend events, participate in discussions, and share your knowledge.

4. **Seek Feedback:** Ask for feedback from colleagues and mentors to understand how you are perceived and where you can improve.

5. **Stay Authentic:** Authenticity is crucial. Be genuine in your interactions and stay true to your values.

Personal branding is an essential tool for leaders in the workplace. It helps build trust, enhances visibility, and opens up opportunities for career growth. Leaders like Shah Rukh Khan demonstrate how a strong personal brand can lead to success and influence in various fields. By focusing on your strengths, being consistent, and staying authentic, you can build a personal brand that sets you apart and leads to long-term success.

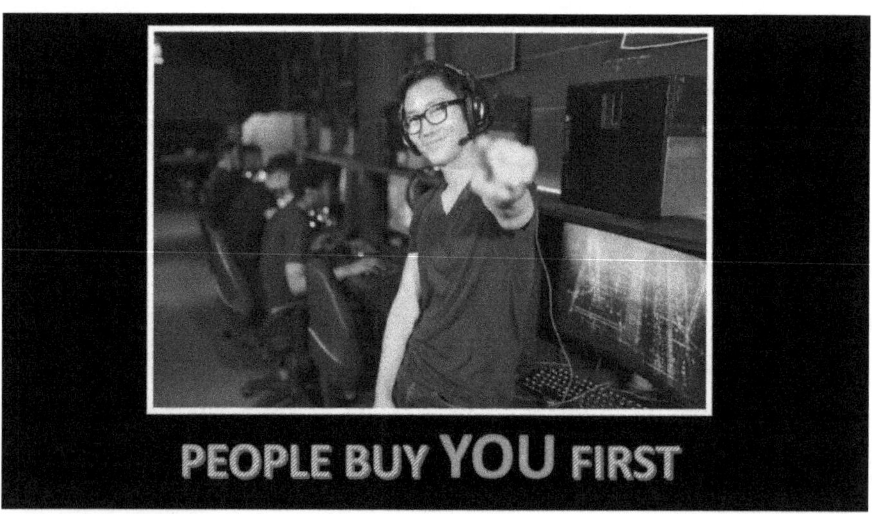

Please remember that people will buy you first. People are always fascinated to buy the branded product. If you can make your brand very strong then you will be sold in the market very easily and at a higher price. Here I want to mean that you can increase your demand in the industry and good organizations will be willing to hire you at a higher package and at a higher position. So, building a strong personal brand is of utmost essential to become a successful leader.

Let me explain to you in a very simple manner that how we can build your own strong brand.

1. **Authenticity**-It means that you need to be authentic always in your activities. Now the question is how you can be authentic always. For this, your TSA have to be aligned always in a straight line.

Let me explain to you. Here

T – Represents thoughts

S – Represents speech

A – Represents action

When your thought, speech and action are in straight line You become authentic to the world. It means that what you think, say accordingly and act accordingly.

But you know what is the problem with many leaders who are never successful and people do not believe them from their core of heart because their TSA is not aligned in a straight line.

They think something, say something different and act just opposite. And they cannot prove themselves as an authentic leader to the world. And people do not trust them.

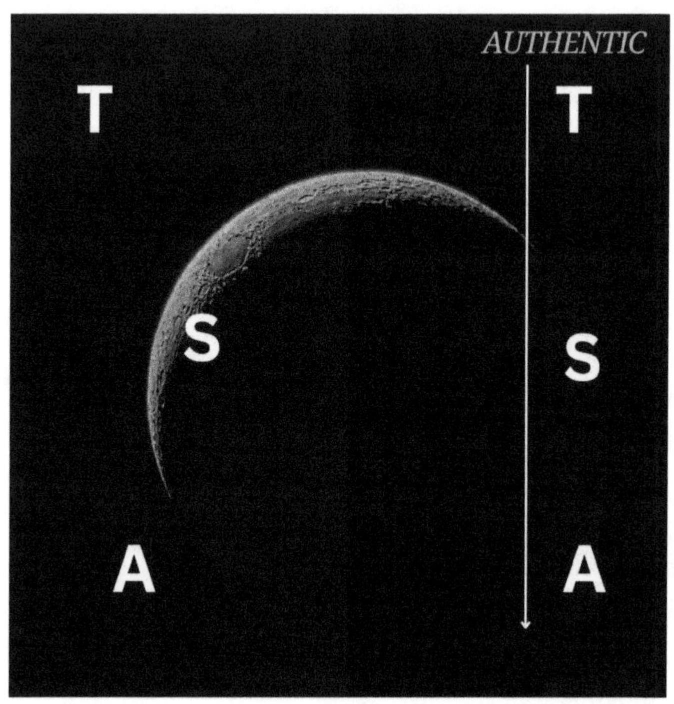

KEEP YOUR TSA ALIGNED IN STRAIGHT LINE

2. Credibility – when you become authentic automatically you build your credibility to the world.

3. Branding – over the time when will build your credibility in the market, towards your team members your colleagues your seniors your juniors in fact to the world you automatically become a strong brand. And people will love to be associated with you from the core of their heart and they will become your die heart fan.

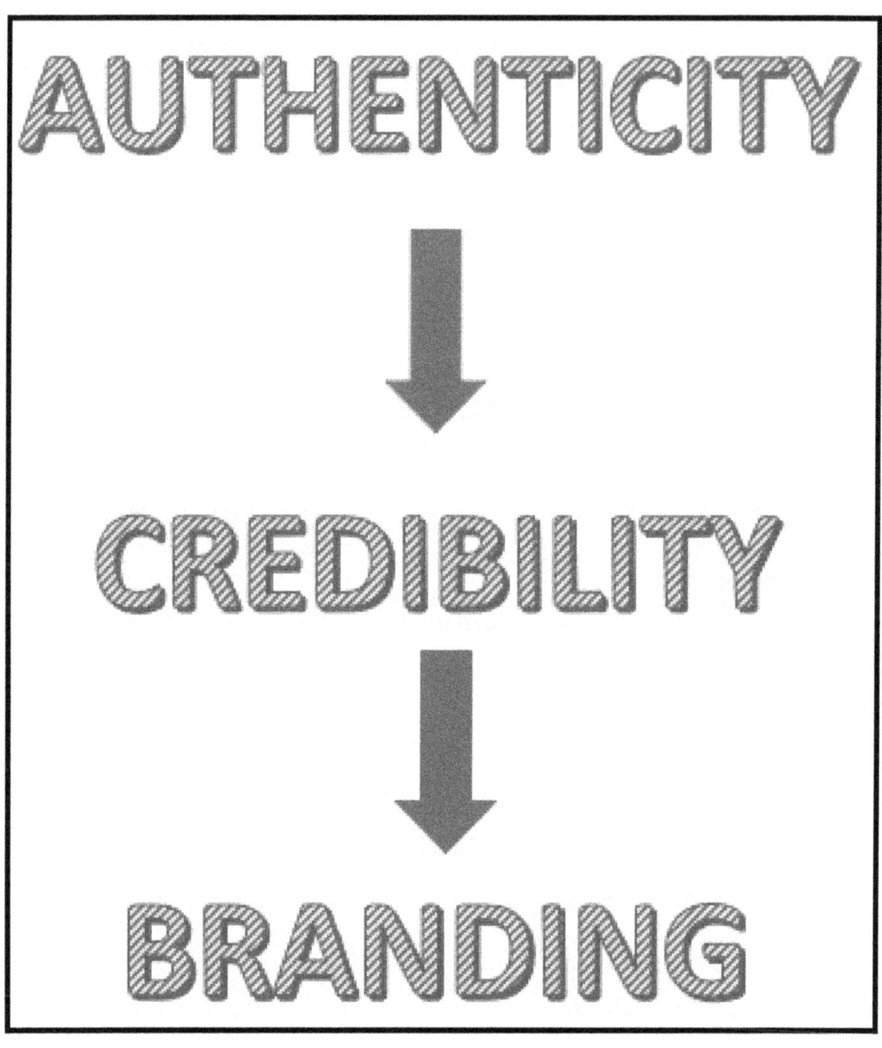

I believe that we have understood the 3 steps to make our own personal brand that is authenticity, which strengthens credibility which ultimately leads to branding.

Now let me give you a formula through which you can easily make your brand as fast as possible.

This is known as 4 C formula. Let me explain these 4 Cs

C – CONNECTION – you need to make a strong connection with people around you. Now when I say a connection it is not a surface to surface connection rather it has to be core to core connection that is heart to heart connection. This can be done through your gesture, body language, empathy. Once you are connected with people from the core through your authenticity people will start liking you and they love to be associated with you and they become your fan. Now they are ready to follow you blindly.

C – COMMUNICATION – the next step is communication. You need to communicate with your team members, your colleagues and your seniors on a continuous basis so that they feel connected with you. This may be through written, verbal or through positive body language or even through social media.

C-CONVERSION – Once you are connected with people and communicate positively they will automatically be converted to your big fans and followers. They will love to work for you willingly and from their hearts and it will be very very easy for you to manage them and achieve organizational goals both qualitative as well as quantitative.

C – COMMUNITY – this is how you can bring all your team members into your own community. They will love to work with you not only in this organization but wherever you go. Because it has been found that many people leave their job not for the organization but for their boss. When you can bring them into your community, you become the most lovable boss for them.

Use this 4C formula to make your successful personal brand.

Bonus Tips: BE A THIEF But the question is what you need to steal?

Steal the "Hearts of Millions

In the following chapters will be discussing the detail action steps to become a celebrity leader.

Primary Role of a Leader: Guiding with Purpose"

Let us see what you have as a leader, no matter at what level you are in

- **More Money – Little anyway**
- **More Fringe Benefit.**
- **Lot More Responsibility.**

What you don't have

- **Freedom to Worry Only About Yourself**
- **Overtime**
- **The Right to Forget About the Job Even When You Go Home**

Why Are Managers Paid More Money?

And What Does A Leader Do to Earn It?

Easy Answer

- A Plumber Fixes Pipes
- A Carpenter Cuts Wood
- A Bricklayer Lays Bricks
- A Salesperson Sells Things
- An Accountant Counts Things
- **A Manager Manages People**

It is harder to manage people than to fix pipes, cut wood, lay bricks or to count things, because people are infinitely more complex

In the organization leaders are found in 3 levels namely lower level leaders, middle level leaders and the top-level leaders.

No matter at what level you are, the leaders should possess 3 primary skills

1. Technical skill

2. Human relations skill

3. Conceptual skill

Technical skills mean the operational skills depending on which department or area you are working.

Human relations skills mean how you can deal and manage with people be it your superior, subordinates or your Peers.

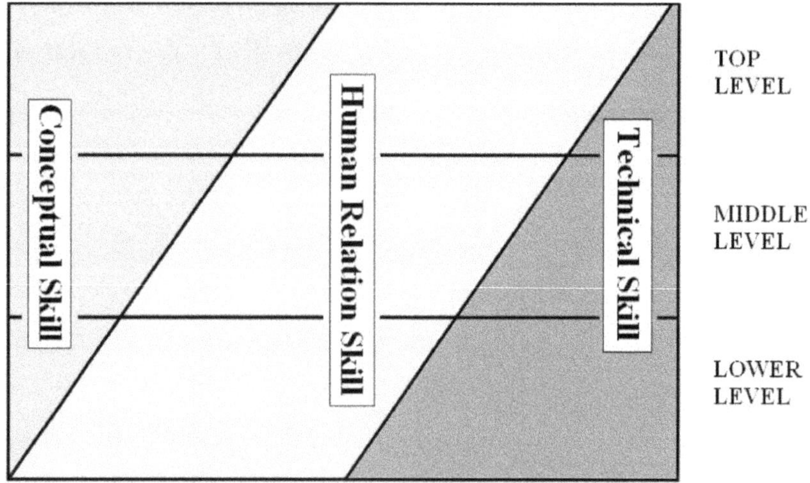

If you observe the above picture very carefully which is the result of a research, you will find that lower level leaders need the maximum amount of technical skills then human relation skill and little amount of conceptual skill.

 HOW TO BECOME A CELEBRITY LEADER IN HOSPITALITY INDUSTRY

The middle level leaders need little less technical skill and little more conceptual skills and also human relation skills.

And lastly the top-level leaders require very little technical skills and more conceptual skills and of course the human relation skills.

The surprising result of this research shows that no matter at which level you are in as a leader, your human relation skill is of prime importance at all levels. It shows that human relation skill is so important in managing people. In fact, human relations skill is most important and priority skill to become a successful leader which with time will make you celebrity leader and you can increase your fan followers day by day.

Your seniors, especially your juniors will love to be associated with you and they will produce the positive result from there within.

What is involved in managing people

To be an effective Leader you have to be a……

1. Psychologist: Understanding the Mental State of Team Members

In the hospitality industry, where employees are constantly interacting with guests, the mental well-being of team members directly impacts service quality. For instance, at the Ritz-Carlton, a key part of their leadership approach is understanding and supporting the emotional state of their employees. Leaders at Ritz-Carlton often engage in one-on-one conversations with their team members to gauge their mood and mental state. By doing this, they ensure that employees feel valued and supported, which in turn enhances their productivity and the guest experience. The result is a workforce that is motivated and happy, leading to higher levels of customer satisfaction.

2. Cheerleader: Spreading Positivity

Positivity in the workplace is infectious, and leaders in the hospitality industry must set the tone. A great example is Richard Branson, founder of Virgin Hotels. Branson is known for his cheerful and energetic leadership style. He believes that by being enthusiastic and positive, a leader can inspire their team to deliver their best work. At Virgin Hotels, this cheerfulness starts from the top and filters down through the entire team, creating a vibrant work environment where employees feel motivated to go the extra mile for guests. This approach leads to an engaged and enthusiastic team, which is reflected in the exceptional guest experiences that Virgin Hotels is known for.

3. Friend: Being Accessible and Approachable

In the hospitality industry, where teamwork is essential, leaders who are friendly and approachable create a supportive environment. Take the example of Arne Sorenson, the late CEO of Marriott International. Sorenson was known for his approachable and down-to-earth leadership style. He made it a point to be accessible to employees at all levels, often visiting hotels and interacting with staff directly. This approach made employees feel comfortable seeking his guidance and sharing their concerns, which fostered a strong sense of camaraderie and trust within the organization. As a result, Marriott employees felt empowered to perform their best, knowing they had a supportive leader who was always available to help.

4. Teacher: Fostering Continuous Learning

The hospitality industry requires constant learning and skill development to keep up with evolving guest expectations. At Four Seasons Hotels and Resorts, leadership is heavily focused on teaching and development. Leaders at Four Seasons are not just managers; they are mentors who take an active role in the professional growth of their team members. For example, they regularly conduct training sessions and workshops to help employees develop new skills and refine existing ones. This focus on continuous learning ensures that employees are well-equipped to handle any challenge, leading to high levels of competence and confidence. Employees who feel supported in their growth are more likely to stay loyal to the company and deliver exceptional service.

5. Taskmaster: Leading by Example

In the hospitality industry, leaders must demonstrate a strong work ethic and a commitment to excellence. An example of this is seen at Hyatt Hotels, where leaders are expected to be role models for their teams. Mark Hoplamazian, CEO of Hyatt Hotels, is known for his hands-on leadership style. He emphasizes the importance of continuous learning and personal development, not just for employees, but for himself as well. By continuously striving to improve and demonstrating a strong work ethic, Hoplamazian sets a high standard for his team members to follow. This leadership approach encourages employees to push their boundaries and achieve their full potential, knowing that their leader is right there with them, setting the pace.

6. Listener: Valuing Team Input

Good leaders in the hospitality industry understand the importance of listening to their team members, as these employees are often the closest to the guests and the operational realities of the business. A notable example is the leadership approach at Hilton Hotels. Chris Nassetta, the CEO of Hilton, has been praised for his listening skills. He regularly holds town hall meetings and open forums where employees can voice their opinions, share ideas, and raise concerns. This open line of communication helps Hilton's leadership stay connected with the front-line employees and ensures that their insights are taken into consideration when making decisions. By being a good listener, Nassetta fosters a culture of inclusion and respect, which leads to higher employee satisfaction and better service delivery.

These examples from the hospitality industry illustrate how effective leaders embody these six qualities—acting as psychologists, cheerleaders, friends, teachers, taskmasters, and listeners—to create a positive and productive work environment. By doing so, they not only enhance their team's performance but also contribute to the overall success of their organization.

BE A HUMAN ENGINEER

We need to follow 2 basic actions

1. **Follow the lay low principles of management**-which includes 3 principles which every leader wants to be absolutely successful needs to follow meticulously.

2. **Follow 10 cardinal rules** – Every leader should consciously avoid these 10 actions. Unfortunately, I have seen that most of the managers who feel they are the leaders use these 10 actions very often in their workplace which leads them to disaster.

In this chapter, we will discuss 3 lay low principles of management and in the next chapter will be discussing 10 cardinal rules.

Lay low principles of management

1. **Stay Calm** – I am sure that all of us have seen swan swimming in the lake. If you observe carefully you will see their face is so calm and tensionless, as if they are enjoying their swimming thoroughly. But if you see underneath you will find they are paddling like a devil. It shows, they are absolutely focused and serious in their actions but on the surface, they are very calm and tensionless.

Every leader, needs to learn this characteristic from the swan. They need to be absolutely focused on their action and work on it like a devil but on the surface, they should be calm and tensionless. This is because, team members are likely to follow their leaders and if they find their leaders are tensed, the team members automatically become tensed which will affect the productivity both qualitative as well as quantitative.

Just like a swan gliding gracefully across a lake, leaders in the hospitality industry must maintain a calm and composed demeanour on the surface, even when they are paddling furiously beneath. This ability to project calmness, while remaining intensely focused on the tasks at hand, is crucial for effective leadership. The swan's example is particularly relevant in the high-pressure environment of the hospitality industry, where maintaining composure can make all the difference in how a team performs under stress.

Ritz-Carlton's Leadership Approach

One of the most iconic examples of this principle in the hospitality industry is the leadership approach at Ritz-Carlton. The hotel chain is known for its impeccable service, which is largely a result of how its leaders handle stress and manage their teams. At Ritz-Carlton, leaders are trained to stay calm and composed, no matter how chaotic the situation might be behind the scenes. This is especially important during high-pressure situations, such as when the hotel is fully booked, or during large events when the staff is stretched to their limits.

For instance, during the preparation for a high-profile event, there might be numerous last-minute changes and unexpected challenges, such as VIP guests requiring special accommodations or unforeseen technical issues. The managers at Ritz-Carlton ensure that they remain calm and composed while addressing these challenges. They work diligently and efficiently behind the scenes, coordinating with various departments, troubleshooting problems, and ensuring everything runs smoothly. However, they do so with a calm exterior, providing clear and reassuring instructions to their team members.

By maintaining a calm demeanour, these leaders create a stable and positive work environment, even under pressure. This calmness is contagious; when team members see their leaders handling stress with grace, they are more likely to remain calm themselves, which helps maintain high standards of service. The result is a seamless guest experience, where the team delivers outstanding service without showing any signs of the challenges they might be facing behind the scenes.

Four Seasons' Guest Recovery

Another example can be seen at Four Seasons Hotels and Resorts, where leaders are taught the importance of staying calm, especially during guest recovery situations. Guest recovery is the process of handling a complaint or issue that a guest has brought forward. It's a critical moment where the hotel's reputation is on the line.

Imagine a scenario where a guest has had a less-than-satisfactory experience—perhaps their room wasn't ready upon arrival, or there was a mix-up with their reservation. The leader in charge must remain calm and composed when addressing the guest's concerns. At Four Seasons, managers are trained to listen empathetically, acknowledge the guest's frustration, and then work quickly behind the scenes to resolve the issue, whether that means offering a complimentary service, upgrading the room, or providing a personalized gesture to make amends.

Behind the scenes, the manager may be coordinating with housekeeping, front desk staff, and other departments to ensure the issue is resolved promptly. They may be juggling multiple tasks, such as rebooking the guest's room, arranging for a special welcome amenity, and updating the guest's profile to prevent similar issues in the future. However, on the surface, they remain calm, collected, and focused solely on making the guest feel valued and taken care of.

This calm approach helps to defuse any tension and reassures the guest that their concerns are being handled by capable hands. It also sets an example for the rest of the staff, showing them how to handle stressful situations without becoming flustered or anxious. As a result, the team can work together effectively, and the guest's experience is salvaged, often leaving them more impressed with the hotel's service than they were initially disappointed.

In the fast-paced and often unpredictable world of hospitality, the ability to stay calm while managing complex and stressful situations is a vital leadership skill. Leaders who adopt the characteristics of a swan—focused and hardworking beneath the surface, but calm and composed on the outside—set a powerful example for their teams. This approach not only helps to maintain a positive work environment but also ensures that service quality remains high, even in the face of challenges. By embodying this principle, leaders in the hospitality industry can inspire confidence and resilience in their teams, ultimately leading to better outcomes for both employees and guests.

So, adopt the characteristics of a swan.

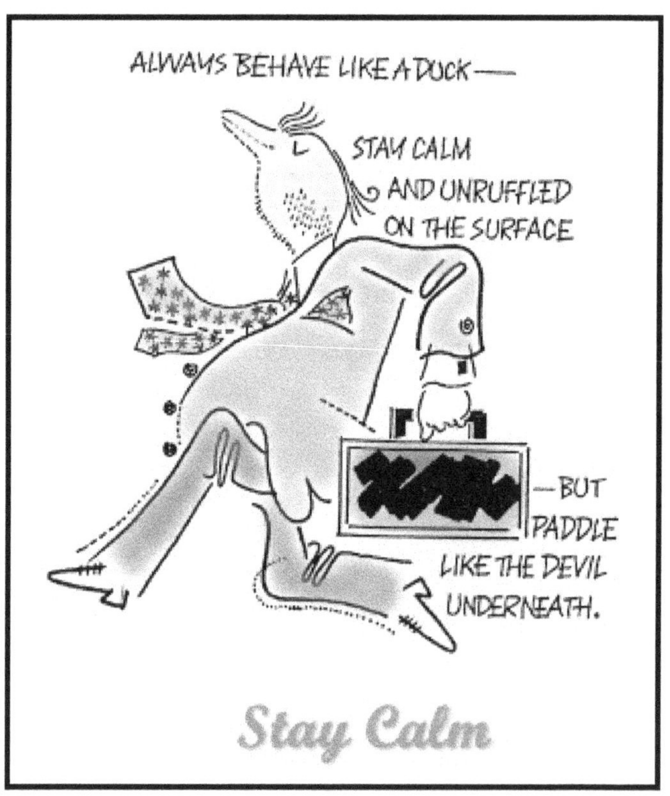

2. **Listen to Team Members** – listening skill is a very important skill for any good leader. It has basically 2 benefits. Number one, you are well informed about the activities in the organization specifically in your domain and number two, you make your team members feel that they are also important part in the organization.

The Importance of Listening Skills for a Leader in the Workplace

Listening is a fundamental skill for any leader. Effective listening enables leaders to understand the needs, concerns, and ideas of their team members, fostering a collaborative and productive work environment. While the benefits of good listening skills are numerous, there are also potential drawbacks that leaders should be aware of to maintain a balanced approach.

Pros of Listening Skills for Leaders

1. Enhanced Communication: Listening actively helps leaders gather accurate information, clarify misunderstandings, and ensure that all team members are on the same page. This leads to better decision-making and problem-solving.

2. Increased Trust and Respect: When leaders listen to their team members, it shows that they value their opinions and contributions. This builds trust and respect, which are essential for a cohesive and motivated team.

3. Improved Employee Engagement: Employees who feel heard are more likely to be engaged and committed to their work. They are more likely to share their ideas and take initiative, leading to innovation and improved performance.

4. Conflict Resolution: Effective listening can help leaders identify the root causes of conflicts and address them constructively. By understanding different perspectives, leaders can mediate disputes and foster a harmonious work environment.

5. Personal Growth and Learning: Listening to others provides leaders with diverse viewpoints and insights, contributing to their personal growth and development. It helps leaders stay open-minded and adaptable in a rapidly changing business landscape.

Cons of Listening Skills for Leaders

1. Time-Consuming: Active listening requires time and patience. Leaders may find it challenging to balance listening with their other responsibilities, especially in fast-paced environments where quick decisions are needed.

2. Information Overload: Leaders who listen to everyone all the time may be overwhelmed by the sheer volume of information. This can lead to difficulty in prioritizing issues and making timely decisions.

3. Perceived Indecisiveness: Leaders who focus too much on listening may be perceived as indecisive or lacking authority. It's important for leaders to strike a balance between listening and taking decisive action.

4. Emotional Drain: Constantly listening to team members' concerns and problems can be emotionally draining for leaders. This can lead to burnout if not managed properly.

5. Potential for Bias: Even the most well-intentioned leaders can fall prey to confirmation bias, where they favour information that aligns with their preconceptions. Leaders need to be aware of this and strive to listen objectively.

Consider the example of Indra Nooyi, the former CEO of PepsiCo. Known for her exceptional listening skills, Nooyi made it a point to listen to her employees, customers, and stakeholders. She often spent time with frontline employees to understand their challenges and gather insights. This approach not only helped her make informed decisions but also earned her immense respect and loyalty from her team. Nooyi's ability to listen effectively played a significant role in her successful leadership and the growth of PepsiCo.

Another great example is Ratan Tata, the former Chairman of Tata Sons. Ratan Tata is renowned for his humility and exceptional listening skills. Throughout his tenure, he made it a point to engage with employees at all levels, from senior executives to factory workers. He would often visit Tata Group's various companies and spend time listening to the challenges and suggestions of the employees.

1. Open-Door Policy: Ratan Tata implemented an open-door policy, encouraging employees to share their ideas and concerns directly with him. This approach not only made employees feel valued but also provided him with diverse perspectives, which were crucial for making informed decisions.

2. Handling Crises: During the Tata Nano crisis, when the project faced significant challenges, Ratan Tata actively listened to the concerns of his team, suppliers, and customers. His willingness to understand different viewpoints helped navigate the crisis and eventually launch the product successfully.

3. Corporate Social Responsibility: Ratan Tata's focus on listening extended beyond the company to the communities Tata Group served. His emphasis on understanding the needs and concerns of local communities led to impactful corporate social responsibility initiatives, enhancing the company's reputation and relationship with society.

By building a culture of listening, Ratan Tata fostered trust, innovation, and loyalty within the Tata Group. His leadership style exemplifies how effective listening can lead to successful and respected leadership.

Listening skills are a vital component of effective leadership in the workplace. They enhance communication, build trust, improve employee engagement, aid in conflict resolution, and contribute to personal growth. However, leaders must be mindful of the potential downsides, such as time constraints, information overload, and emotional drain. By balancing listening with decisive action, leaders can harness the full benefits of this crucial skill while mitigating its drawbacks. Leaders like Ratan Tata demonstrate how effective listening can lead to successful and respected leadership.

Please Remember

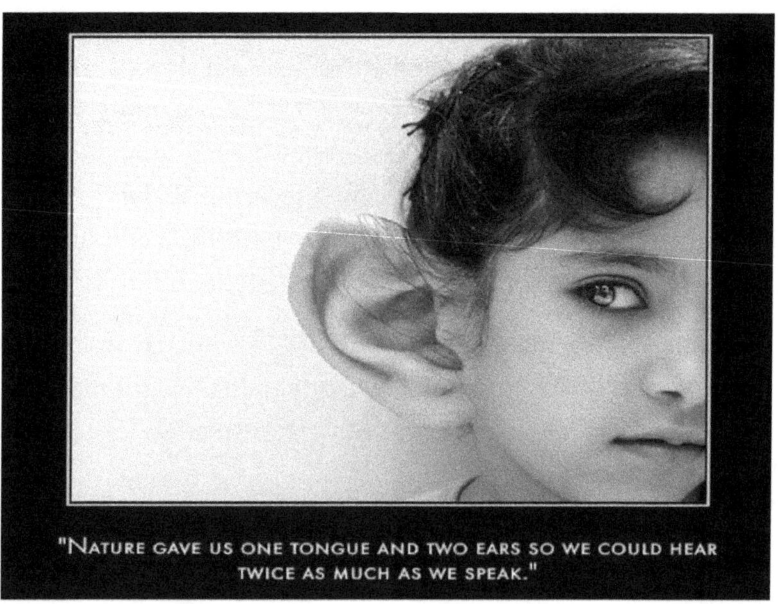

3. Say As Little As Possible

"Say as little as possible" is often attributed to the idea of thoughtful communication. For a successful leader, this means choosing words carefully, speaking with intention, and listening more than talking. This approach can enhance clarity, build trust, and prevent misunderstandings. However, there are also potential drawbacks to consider. Let's explore the benefits and challenges of this communication strategy in the corporate workplace.

Benefits of Saying As Little As Possible

1. Clarity and Precision: Leaders who speak concisely are often clearer and more precise. This helps in delivering messages effectively without leaving room for misinterpretation. Example: Sundar Pichai, CEO of Alphabet Inc., is known for his clear and concise communication. His ability to simplify complex ideas has been crucial in aligning teams across Google's vast operations.

2. Enhanced Listening: By saying less, leaders create space for others to speak, fostering an environment where team members feel heard and valued. This can lead to better understanding and more informed decision-making.

   Example: Satya Nadella, CEO of Microsoft, emphasizes active listening. His leadership style has been credited with transforming Microsoft's culture to be more inclusive and innovative.

3. Authority and Respect: Speaking less can also convey authority and confidence. When leaders choose their words carefully, it shows that they are thoughtful and measured, which can command respect from their team.

4. Reducing Errors: Less talk reduces the risk of saying something inappropriate or making hasty decisions. Careful speech minimizes the chance of mistakes that could lead to misunderstandings or conflicts.

Problems of Speaking (Babbling) Too Much

1. Dilution of Message: Talking too much can dilute the main message, making it harder for people to grasp the key points. Over-explaining can lead to confusion and loss of focus. Example: A leader in a meeting who keeps elaborating on every detail might lose the audience's attention, making it difficult for them to retain important information.

2. Perceived Lack of Confidence: Over-talking can be perceived as a lack of confidence. Leaders who feel the need to explain every detail or justify their decisions excessively might appear unsure of themselves.

3. Limited Listening: Leaders who dominate conversations leave little room for others to contribute. This can stifle creativity and innovation, as team members might feel their ideas are not valued or considered.

4. Potential Miscommunication: Speaking too much increases the likelihood of saying something that could be misinterpreted or taken out of context, leading to misunderstandings and potential conflicts.

   Example: A manager who frequently changes their instructions during a project can confuse the team, resulting in mistakes and inefficiency.

5. Wasting Time: Excessive talking can waste valuable time, especially in meetings. This can reduce productivity and frustrate team members who prefer to focus on action rather than lengthy discussions.

"Saying as little as possible" in the corporate workplace emphasizes the value of thoughtful and intentional communication. Successful leaders like Sundar Pichai and Satya Nadella exemplify how concise and active listening can lead to clarity, better understanding, and enhanced team dynamics. However, leaders must also be mindful of the balance required, as too little communication can lead to a lack of guidance, while too much can dilute messages and create confusion. By striking the right balance, leaders can foster an environment of respect, innovation, and efficiency, driving their teams and organizations towards success.

 **10**

Ten Cardinal Rules – A Leader Should Not Practice

1. Prioritize the Mission, Not the Ego – Don't Make An Ego Trip

It's important not to charge in like Mr. Jack of all trades, ready to toss out all the old rules and procedures, proclaiming, "Things will be DIFFERENT now that I'm in charge."

You must have heard this kind of statement from the leader very often.

"See I have more than 20 years' experience in international brands & we used to work differently.

Here I see, you all are outdated but don't worry I have come, I will teach you all modern techniques.

First, forget all your old ideas"

People start thinking, hey lord,then what we are doing for so many years? This man is saying we all are wrong. Then how we survived for all these years?

Please remember, people resist changes. So, take time to change present practices if required.

Certainly, change is inevitable, but many existing rules and procedures have been carefully crafted over time for specific reasons. For instance, workplace safety protocols might have evolved to prevent accidents based on past incidents. Therefore, before making sweeping changes, it's crucial to understand why things are done the way they are. For example, modifying shift schedules without considering workload patterns could disrupt productivity. Thus, a thoughtful approach to change ensures that improvements are made without unintended negative impacts.

Certainly some things are going to be different, but many others got the way they are for good reason. Until you know for sure why they are being done that way it makes sense to be very careful about changing them.

Don't Make An Ego Trip

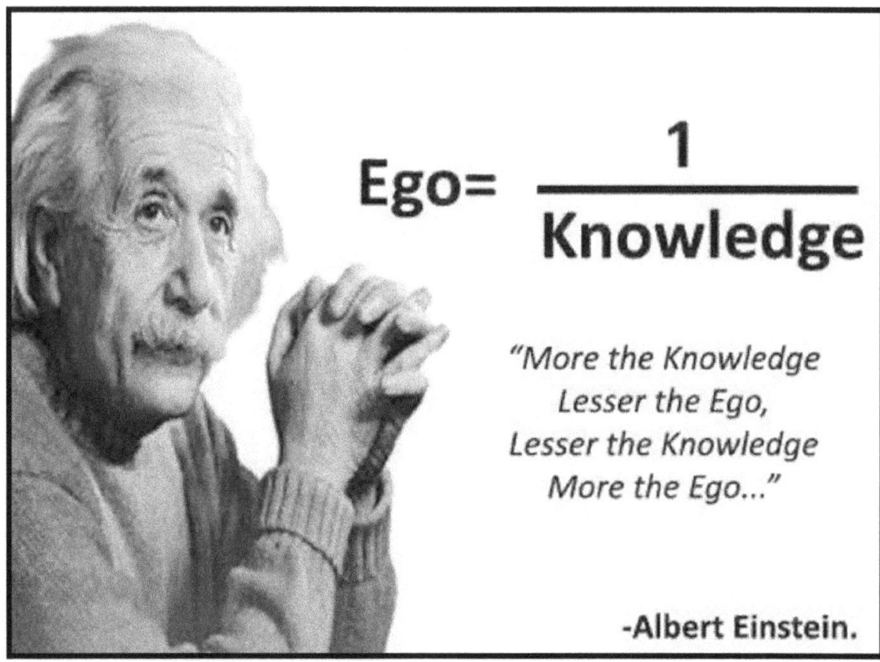

2. Commit Wisely, Deliver Surely – Don't Make Careless Promises

First, you can't buy friendship or loyalty. For example, in the hotel industry, giving employees bonuses or expensive gifts might not earn their genuine respect or long-term dedication. True loyalty comes from fair treatment, good working conditions, and mutual trust, not from material incentives.

Second, never promise anything you aren't absolutely certain you can deliver. For instance, if you promise your staff more vacation days or a raise without being sure you can provide it, you risk losing their trust when you can't follow through.

Third, rewards should be handed out very slowly, if at all, until you get your feet under you and know exactly who is deserving of rewards. For example, when you first start managing a hotel, take your time to observe your staff. You might find that the housekeeping supervisor who consistently maintains high standards of cleanliness deserves recognition more than someone who initially seems impressive but lacks consistency.

Fourth, rewards should be handed out only for what people have done in the past and what they are going to continue to do in the future. For instance, you might reward a front desk employee who has consistently provided excellent customer service and shows a commitment to maintaining this high level of performance. This approach ensures that rewards are meaningful and motivate continued excellence.

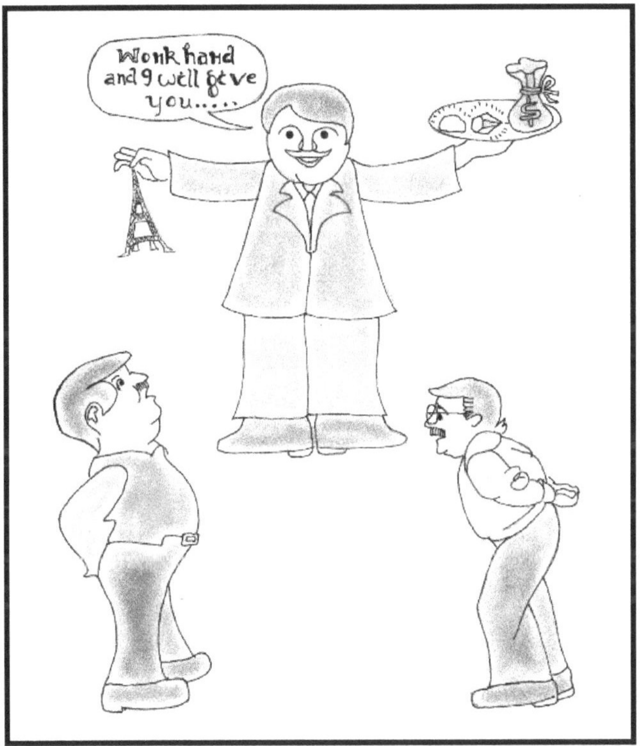

Don't Make Careless Promises

3. Lead with Compassion, Not Conquest – Don't Play Genghis Khan

Interestingly, acting like a tyrant is more likely to reveal your insecurities than your strengths. For example, if you start ordering your hotel staff around as if they were slaves, you will create unnecessary enemies.

Imagine treating your front desk clerks harshly, demanding they follow every instruction without question; this will lead to resentment and a hostile work environment. In extreme cases, you might face a staff revolt, which would hardly convince your boss that you are a competent leader.

True power is often displayed in a quiet, firm manner. For instance, if you calmly and confidently assign tasks to your housekeeping team, taking for granted that your orders will be followed, you will foster a respectful and cooperative atmosphere. Believing in your authority and treating your employees with respect will naturally lead them to acknowledge and respect your leadership. If you trust in your own leadership abilities, your staff will follow suit, leading to a more harmonious and productive hotel environment.

Don't Play Genghis Khan

4. Value Every Voice – Don't Play Favourites

One of the critical characteristics of a good leader is treating all employees fairly. For instance, in the hospitality industry, if you praise or reward only a few favourite staff members, like the front desk manager or head chef, while ignoring others, you will quickly see morale drop among the rest of your team. Imagine being a housekeeping staff member who consistently works hard but never gets recognized because the manager always favours the restaurant staff. Your interest in the job would disappear, and you would feel angry and frustrated. Why put in your best effort if it's always overlooked in favour of someone else?

It's a basic law of human nature—everyone thrives on praise and recognition. In the hospitality industry, whether you're a bellhop, concierge, or part of the cleaning crew, everyone likes to feel special and important. If employees are denied this recognition, they often stop putting in their best effort because they see it as a waste of time and energy. Therefore, as a leader, it's essential to ensure that praise and rewards are distributed fairly to maintain high morale and motivation among all staff members.

During my training program in different corporate houses, I observed there are so many self-proclaimed leaders who love to spend their time into their air-conditioned office rather in the shop floor.

So, to manage their team members they take a shortcut method by appointing few favorites to get the information of the shop floor and accordingly they take a decision. They think they are doing a very right thing by establishing so called MIS ie management information system for them.

But they do not understand these favorites never give the right information rather give the concocted information for their favour and these so-called leaders take decisions accordingly which are absolutely wrong in most of the time.

This is how they lose trust of their team members and invite disaster in the workplace.

I don't know how many of you have seen the famous Hindi film Sholay where the British period jailer used the same technique to acquire information about the activities in the jail and he used to take decision accordingly and all the time he was a super failure.

So, I always suggest visiting the shop floor often and communicating with your team members so that you get the right information about the activities in that department or in the organization. It will be very easy for you to understand the present situation and will be absolutely helpful to take right decision most of the time.

So never ever make your favorites to gather information of the shop floor. If you do so I can guarantee you that you will be absolutely failure leader in the organization.

Don't Play Favourites

5. Speak with Purpose, Not Impulse – Don't Babble Without Thinking

1. **Think Before You Speak**: In the hospitality industry, it's crucial not to speak without thinking. For instance, if you're leading a team meeting at your hotel and casually criticize the way the housekeeping staff handles their tasks without understanding their challenges, it can create unnecessary tension.

2. **Understand Your Influence**: Remember that your staff responds to your position of power, not necessarily to your brilliance. For example, as a hotel manager, your employees might nod and agree with your suggestions, not because they are the best ideas, but because they respect your authority.

3. **Avoid Being Seduced by Attention:** It's easy to get carried away by the attention you receive, especially if you are nervous at the start. For instance, during a busy season, you might find yourself giving spontaneous speeches to motivate your staff. While it's good to communicate, doing so without a clear message can lead to confusion.

4. **Beware of Babbling**: When you're nervous, you might start talking too much without a clear point. Imagine you're addressing your hotel's front desk team and start rambling about various issues without offering concrete solutions. This can confuse your staff and make you seem unprepared.

5. **Consequences of Thoughtless Remarks**: Be aware that your employees will remember and possibly misinterpret your careless comments. For instance, if you jokingly suggest that the kitchen staff is slow, this could spread and lower their morale. Later, this remark could be brought up in staff grievances, causing bigger issues.

    Another example, if you casually mention during a meeting that the night shift doesn't work as hard as the day shift, it can create resentment among the night staff. This remark might get repeated and spread, leading to a divide between the two shifts and lowering overall morale. Later, this comment could be brought up in staff complaints, causing significant issues and requiring you to address and mend the team dynamics.

By following these points and providing clear, thoughtful communication, you can lead your hospitality team effectively and maintain a positive working environment.

Don't Babble Without Thinking

6. Empower Your Team – Don't Hoard The Work

What is Delegation?

Delegation is the process of assigning specific tasks or responsibilities to others while maintaining overall accountability. In a workplace, this means a manager or leader assigns duties to employees, trusting them to complete these tasks effectively and efficiently. Delegation involves not just handing over the task but also providing the necessary resources, guidance, and support to ensure the task is completed successfully.

Why is Delegation Important in the Workplace?

1. Enhances Efficiency: Delegation allows tasks to be completed simultaneously, rather than sequentially. For example, in a hotel, while the manager oversees operations, the housekeeping supervisor can handle room assignments, and the front desk staff can manage check-ins and check-outs. This division of labor ensures that multiple aspects of the business are running smoothly at the same time.

2. Frees Up Time for Strategic Planning: When leaders delegate routine tasks, they free up time to focus on higher-level strategic planning and decision-making. For instance, a hotel manager who delegates daily operational tasks can focus on marketing strategies, improving guest services, or expanding the hotel's facilities.

3. Empowers Employees: Delegation empowers employees by giving them more responsibility and opportunities to develop their skills. For example, assigning a team member the task of organizing a corporate event helps them learn event planning and coordination, which can boost their confidence and career development.

4. Builds Trust and Morale: When managers delegate tasks, it shows that they trust their employees' abilities. This trust can significantly improve employee morale and job satisfaction. For instance, when a hotel manager entrusts a front desk employee with handling VIP guest check-ins, it demonstrates confidence in their skills, which can increase the employee's commitment to their role.

5. Improves Team Collaboration: Delegation encourages collaboration and teamwork. When tasks are shared among employees, they must communicate and work together to achieve common goals. For instance, in a restaurant within a hotel, the kitchen staff, waiters, and management need to work in sync to deliver excellent dining experiences.

6. Reduces Burnout: By spreading out the workload, delegation helps prevent burnout among employees. For instance, if one person is handling all guest complaints, they can quickly become overwhelmed. Delegating some of these responsibilities to other team members ensures that no one is overburdened.

7. Develops Future Leaders: Effective delegation is crucial for succession planning. By giving employees more responsibilities and opportunities to lead projects, managers can identify and develop future leaders within the organization. For example, a senior concierge given the responsibility to train new staff can gain leadership skills that prepare them for future managerial roles.

In summary, delegation is a vital management skill that enhances efficiency, empowers employees, builds trust, improves collaboration, reduces burnout, and helps develop future leaders. It's a crucial practice for ensuring a well-functioning and motivated workplace.

Often out of nervousness, impatience, or simply because you don't trust your subordinates to do the job right, you end up trying to do everything yourself. For instance, in the hospitality industry, you might find yourself overseeing the front desk operations, handling guest complaints, managing housekeeping schedules, and even coordinating with the kitchen staff all on your own.

Pretty soon, your desk is stacked with memos waiting for your approval. For example, maintenance requests, event planning

HOW TO BECOME A CELEBRITY LEADER IN HOSPITALITY INDUSTRY

approvals, and staff schedule changes all pile up because you're trying to manage them personally. Decisions don't get made in a timely manner, and work gets backed up. As a result, your hotel or department becomes the bottleneck, slowing down operations and affecting overall efficiency.

This is by no means an unusual problem. Every leader who cares about their work feels an almost overwhelming sense of responsibility. For instance, as a hotel manager, you might think it's easier and faster to handle guest reservations yourself rather than showing a new front desk employee how to do it properly.

However, training and delegation are among your most important responsibilities as a leader. Delegation means assigning tasks and responsibilities to your employees, trusting them to handle these duties. For example, you could delegate the task of organizing a large event to your experienced event coordinator or assign a senior housekeeper the responsibility of managing daily cleaning schedules.

Neglecting delegation invites disaster. Without delegation, you overburden yourself, important tasks get delayed, and your staff doesn't get the opportunity to grow and take on more responsibilities. By effectively delegating, you ensure that your hotel runs smoothly, decisions are made promptly, and your employees feel trusted and valued, which boosts their morale and efficiency.

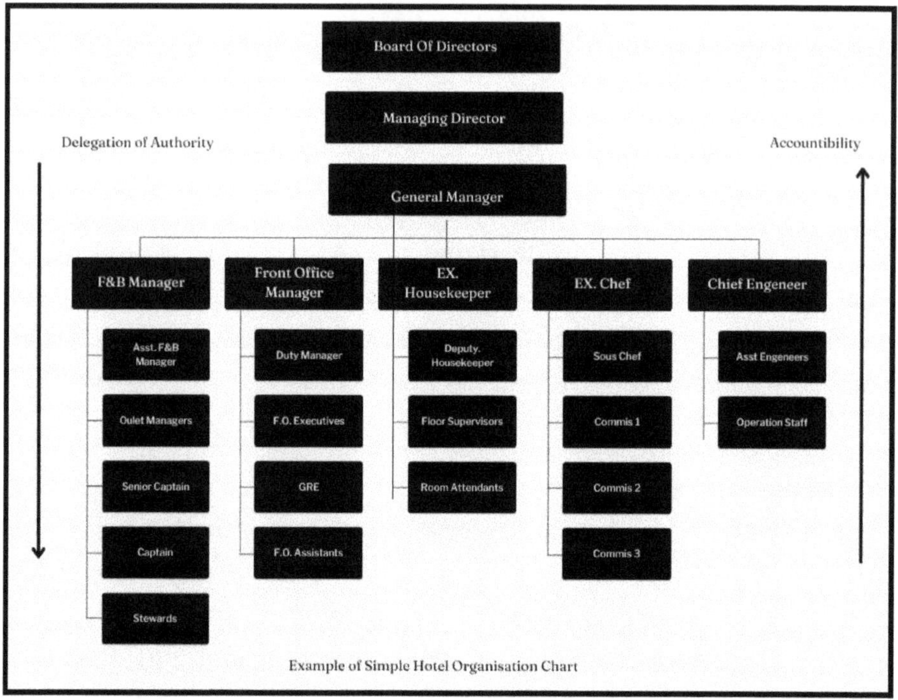

Example of Simple Hotel Organisation Chart

Through the above organizational chart let me explain how delegation works in the organization.

Please understand that we cannot delegate the responsibility instead we need to delegate the authority along with the responsibility to complete the task.

First let us understand what is authority. Authority means the power of taking decisions and making orders to others to execute the decision.

If you go through the above organizational chart you will find on top there are board of directors below board of directors there is a managing director below managing director there is a general manager and under the general manager there are head of the departments. Under each head of the department there are many subordinates which are explained in the above chart.

Now, the final authority has been centralized in the hands of the board of directors but board of directors cannot take all the decisions required in the organization that is the reason they delegate some of their authority to the next level that is to the managing director. Similarly managing director also cannot take all the decisions and because of that reasons he delegates some of his authority to the general manager. This is how the authority comes down from top to bottom step by step. It means everybody in the organization must have some amount of authority whether big or small to take the decisions in their own area. So delegation of authority is the downward force which flows from top to bottom.

Now, when someone receive the authority from his immediate superior he becomes responsible to perform certain duties and automatically he becomes accountable, answerable, questionable for his performance to his immediate superior from whom he received authority.

So, accountability is an upward force which exist in the organization. The most important thing is this the delegation of authority has to be balanced with the upward force that is accountability. So, these two forces of delegation of authority and accountability binds the organization so that everybody can perform their duties towards their goal.

That is why it is said " **Delegate But Do Not Abdicate"**

So, never delegate only responsibility. Responsibility has to be delegated along with the proper authority so that every person can function in their own area effectively.

I have seen many general managers those who issue circulars and at the bottom writes " all are concerned"

It clearly means to the people that no one is concerned. Because everybody thinks if all are concerned then someone will execute and I don't need to involve myself into that.

Let me tell you an old interesting story.

There was a king who had a wish to have a milk pond in his Kingdom. One day he called a general meeting with all the people of his Kingdom and expressed his wish. He said, to do this I need help from all of you. Everybody said loudly my Lord, tell us what can we do? We are ready to give our life for you.

The king said next Thursday during New moon, excavation of new pond will be ready and you all come in the midnight to pour one small Pot of milk in the pond.

On Thursday midnight, everybody lined up with a pot in their hand as per the king's directives.

Everybody thought, others are pouring milk and if I pour a pot of water, nobody will know.

So actually, everybody poured water into the pond thinking the others were pouring a milk.

The king already instructed everybody to come sharp at 9:00 in the morning on Friday to inaugurate the milk pond.

But when everybody assembled there, all have seen the pond is full of water and there was no milk.

The king said, I knew it and I wanted to a test your loyalty that is the reason I asked all of you to pour milk in the midnight and that too in a new moon.

This is a common human nature. So, when the leader said everybody is concerned, the people think that others will take the responsibility why should I take only and ultimately nobody takes the responsibility. That is why, you need to delegate the authority along with the responsibility to the right people so that you can hold him accountable for the execution.

 HOW TO BECOME A CELEBRITY LEADER IN HOSPITALITY INDUSTRY

Don't Hoard The Work. Buzz Word Is Delegation

Please remember while delegating, you must understand your priorities.

7. Own Your Actions – Don't Pass the Buck

A key rule of good management is to own your actions. If things go wrong in your area, it's your fault. If things go right, it's because of the people who report to you. For example, if a hotel guest has a bad experience due to a mistake at the front desk, a good manager should take responsibility rather than blaming the front desk staff. Conversely, if a guest has an exceptional stay because of the attentiveness of the housekeeping team, the manager should give credit to those team members.

When a manager tries to shift the blame to employees, it damages trust and respect. Imagine a situation where a restaurant in the hotel receives complaints about slow service. If the manager blames the waitstaff publicly, it not only demoralizes them but also makes them less likely to take initiative in the future.

Loyalty is a two-way street. If you want your staff to be loyal and committed to you, you need to show them the same level of loyalty and support. For instance, if a kitchen mishap occurs, standing by your culinary team and working together to solve the issue builds a stronger team bond.

Remember, credit multiplies, blame divides. When you give credit to your team for their hard work, it motivates them and fosters a positive work environment. For example, publicly praising the event coordinator for a flawlessly executed conference can boost the morale of the entire events team. On the other hand, assigning blame creates divisions and resentment, which can disrupt team cohesion and overall performance.

Let me quote a famous speech of Dr. APJ Abdul Kalam which is the apt example of the above.

"Today is 17th August 1979, and I am the mission director and project director. We are all in the control centre. The computer takes over at T minus eight minutes, which means the computer takes control. At T minus four minutes, the computer protocol says 'Don't launch.' I immediately put the rocket in manual mode. The rocket took off, and for the first 100 seconds, it was a beautiful launch. But soon, I knew we had lost the rocket system. Within a few seconds, instead of putting the satellite into orbit, the whole system went into the Bay of Bengal. I was the mission director and project director. I had failed.

About 5,000 people had worked on the mission, but the chairman of the Indian Space Research Organization took responsibility for the failure. He completely shifted my failure to his failure. Exactly one year later, I took the mic and announced to all the stations, 'Here is your mission director. The satellite is in orbit, and we congratulate you.' I told them."

This speech captures the essence of leadership and taking responsibility, exemplified by APJ Abdul Kalam and his chairman at ISRO.

Own Your Actions – Don't Pass The Buck

8. Stay Emotionally Balanced – Don't Throw Temper Tantrums

A sure sign of childish behaviour is losing your temper by shouting, screaming, pounding the desk, throwing things, or swearing. In the hospitality industry, this kind of behavior is particularly damaging. For example, if a hotel manager starts yelling at the housekeeping staff because a room wasn't cleaned on time, it doesn't solve the problem and instead makes the staff feel scared and disrespected.

People don't see this behaviour as tough but simply crazy and untrustworthy. If you continually lose your temper, pretty soon you'll be the last to hear any bad news. For instance, if the kitchen staff knows the manager reacts angrily to mistakes, they might hide problems with a meal service. By the time you find out, it might be too late to fix the issue before it affects guests.

It is your job to solve problems, not create them. This takes incredible patience and self-control. Imagine a situation where a guest complains about a billing error. Instead of reacting angrily towards the front desk employee who made the mistake, a good manager will calmly address the issue and guide the employee on how to avoid such errors in the future.

You don't have to deny your feelings. You wouldn't be human if you didn't get frustrated and angry at times. For example, when there's a last-minute event booking that causes chaos, it's natural to feel stressed. The trick is to direct your frustration or anger at the situation, not at the people. Even if the banquet team is responsible for the oversight, handling the problem calmly and constructively ensures it gets resolved without damaging relationships or morale.

By staying emotionally balanced, you foster a work environment where employees feel respected and supported, leading to better teamwork and more effective problem-solving.

9. Lead by Example, Not Exception – Don't Take Special Privileges

As a leader, you might suddenly have the opportunity to come in late, go home early, take long lunch breaks, or make many personal calls. Feeling important, you might be tempted to use these privileges. However, in the hospitality industry, leading by example is crucial.

Remember, you are constantly being observed by your employees. If you're a hotel manager who frequently arrives late or leaves early, the staff will notice. For example, if you take extended lunch breaks while expecting your team to stick to their strict schedules, it sends a message that you don't value the same discipline you demand from them.

You are an example to the people who report to you. If you don't set a good example, they won't follow. For instance, if the head chef takes personal calls during busy kitchen hours, it might encourage the sous chefs and line cooks to do the same, disrupting the kitchen's efficiency.

You can't expect your team to give 100 percent effort if you're not around to see and appreciate it. Imagine asking your front desk staff to handle a surge of check-ins efficiently while you're frequently absent or disengaged. They might feel undervalued and demotivated.

On the other hand, if you put in extra time and work hard, the message will be clear about what you value and reward. For instance, staying late to help the events team set up for a big conference shows your commitment. When the team sees you working alongside them, it reinforces a culture of dedication and teamwork.

By leading by example, you show your employees that you are part of the team, dedicated to the same goals, and willing to put in the effort required to achieve success. This fosters respect, loyalty, and a strong work ethic throughout the organization.

Please Remember "Your Input Is Your Subordinates Output"

10. Balance Authority with Approachability – Don't Be Too Much of a Company Loyalist or Too Much of a Buddy

As a leader in the hospitality industry, you must balance your loyalty to the company with your loyalty to your employees. If you lean too much toward the company, seeing it as your path to success, your staff might view you as a sycophant. For example, if a hotel manager always sides with upper management without considering staff concerns, the employees might feel undervalued and resentful.

Conversely, if you become too chummy with your staff, maintaining authority becomes challenging. For instance, if a restaurant manager spends too much time socializing with waitstaff and bartenders, it can be hard to enforce rules and expectations when needed. This familiarity might lead to a lack of respect for your authority.

Avoid sharing overly personal details, such as how much you dislike the company or intimate stories from your personal life. For example, telling your staff that you hate working at the hotel and plan to leave as soon as you get another job undermines your leadership. Similarly, sharing details about your personal relationships, like last night's date, can blur professional boundaries.

It's important to understand that old buddy relationships can't be carried into your new role as a leader. For instance, if you were once a bartender promoted to bar manager, you need to maintain a professional distance to ensure respect and effective management. You're the boss now, and with that title comes a certain distance that you need to accept and use wisely.

Balancing authority with approachability means being fair, listening to your team, and supporting them while maintaining clear professional boundaries. For example, a good hotel manager listens to staff concerns about scheduling but makes decisions based on the best interest of both the employees and the hotel. This balanced approach helps build a respectful and productive work environment.

We've discussed what makes a leader and how they should behave, but what does a leader actually do all day?

In the hospitality industry, a leader's primary responsibility is to get the work done through their team. This involves a variety of tasks to ensure smooth operations and excellent service. For instance:

1. **Managing Daily Operations**: A hotel manager oversees the daily operations, ensuring rooms are clean, bookings are managed, and guests are satisfied. They coordinate with the housekeeping team to ensure rooms are ready for new arrivals and work with the front desk to handle guest check-ins and check-outs efficiently.

2. **Ensuring Quality Service**: Leaders make sure guests receive high-quality service. This could involve training the restaurant staff to provide excellent dining experiences or ensuring the spa services meet the highest standards. They might conduct regular team meetings to address any issues and brainstorm ways to enhance guest satisfaction.

3. **Handling Logistics**: Leaders ensure that supplies and resources are available when needed. For example, a banquet manager ensures that all necessary items for an event, such as decorations, food, and equipment, are delivered on time and set up correctly. They also work with vendors to secure the best prices and timely deliveries.

4. **Resolving Issues**: Leaders are problem solvers. If there's a complaint from a guest about their stay, the leader addresses it promptly and effectively. They listen to the guest's concerns, apologize for any inconvenience, and take steps to rectify the situation, ensuring the guest leaves happy.

5. **Supporting the Team:** A good leader supports their team through challenges. If an employee is struggling with a task, the leader provides guidance and support. For instance, if a new concierge is having trouble with guest inquiries, the leader might provide additional training and resources to help them succeed.

Leaders also need to balance personal issues and work responsibilities. While it's important to be empathetic, their main concern is ensuring the job gets done correctly and on time. For example, if an employee is facing personal difficulties, a good leader will offer support but also ensure that the work is not compromised.

The next question is, how does a leader do their job effectively?

A leader does their job by setting clear expectations, delegating tasks appropriately, and maintaining open communication with their team. They use their time wisely, focusing on high-priority tasks and empowering their employees to take ownership of their roles. By leading with efficiency and empathy, they create a positive work environment that drives success and satisfaction for both employees and guests.

Here are Five Effective Habits of A leader for Maximum Impact

1. Prioritize Employee Safety for Optimal Performance

Effectiveness might seem like a buzzword to some, but it has a straightforward meaning: achieving the most with the least effort, money, and time. In the hospitality industry, the most effective way to accomplish tasks is by ensuring safety.

Ensuring safety is not just about avoiding accidents; it's about creating an environment where employees can perform their best without fear of injury or health risks. For example, in a hotel kitchen, ensuring all staff are trained to use equipment correctly and understand fire safety protocols reduces the risk of accidents. A well-maintained kitchen where employees know the proper procedures can operate more efficiently and effectively.

When safety is compromised, costs rise. For instance, if housekeeping staff are not trained to handle cleaning chemicals properly, accidents can occur, leading to injuries and potential lawsuits. This not only affects the well-being of employees but also increases costs for the hotel in terms of medical expenses and legal fees.

Taking chances with the safety or health of your employees will never pay off. Imagine a scenario where the maintenance team is asked to fix a problem with inadequate safety gear. An injury here would not only delay the repair but also demoralize the team and reduce overall productivity. Moreover, unsafe practices can lead to high turnover rates, as employees will not stay loyal to a workplace that doesn't prioritize their well-being.

For instance, ensuring the hotel staff have proper ergonomics training and equipment, such as supportive shoes for long hours of standing or tools to lift heavy luggage, can prevent long-term injuries. Regular safety drills and a clear protocol for emergencies also help in keeping everyone prepared and secure.

In conclusion, prioritizing safety is essential for effective management. It ensures tasks are completed efficiently and fosters a loyal, productive workforce. By making safety a top priority, you create a sustainable work environment where both the employees and the business can thrive.

2. Foster Teamwork for Success

Getting people to work together means fostering cooperation, not using intimidation. In the hospitality industry, this cooperation extends to your team, your superiors, and other departments within the company.

For example, as a hotel manager, you need to collaborate with your housekeeping team to ensure rooms are ready for guests, with the front desk to manage bookings, and with the kitchen staff to handle guest meals efficiently. Cooperation means working together towards a common goal, like providing excellent service to guests, rather than using fear or threats to get things done.

Sometimes, leaders create a strong bond within their work group but struggle to cooperate with other departments. For instance, a restaurant manager might build a close-knit team but have difficulties working with the banquet or housekeeping departments. This can lead to a narrow focus, where the team only prioritizes their own tasks, ignoring the bigger picture and hindering overall growth and success within the hotel.

On the other hand, if a leader pays too much attention to other departments and neglects their own team, the quality and quantity of their group's work can decline. For example, if a hotel manager spends all their time in meetings with upper management and rarely checks in with their staff, the team might feel unsupported and unmotivated, leading to poor performance.

A good leader balances the needs of their team with the needs of the entire organization. They think about what is best for everyone, not just their own group. For instance, a banquet manager should ensure their team is well-prepared for events but also communicate and coordinate with the kitchen staff and front desk to ensure everything runs smoothly.

By maintaining a balance, the leader ensures that their team feels valued and supported while also contributing to the overall success of the organization. This balanced approach fosters a sense of unity and cooperation across the entire company, leading to better performance and higher employee satisfaction.

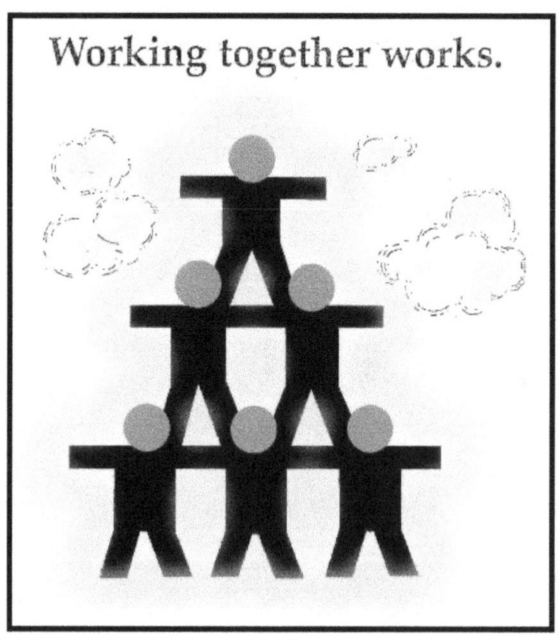

 HOW TO BECOME A CELEBRITY LEADER IN HOSPITALITY INDUSTRY

3. Building and Nurturing Team Spirit

Morale and team spirit are crucial in any group, especially in the hospitality industry. Employees often find it challenging to stay motivated when working towards large, abstract goals like "profits" or "quality." These goals can feel distant and impersonal. Instead, they respond better to immediate rewards, such as praise, recognition, or the satisfaction of working together to achieve something they couldn't accomplish alone.

This is the essence of team spirit. It's exciting, rewarding, and fun. Developing this spirit requires creativity and genuine care. For example, a hotel manager might recognize an outstanding employee of the month with a certificate and a special mention during team meetings. This small act of recognition can boost morale and motivate others to strive for excellence.

Another way to foster team spirit is by celebrating achievements together. For instance, if the hotel receives positive feedback from a guest about the cleanliness and comfort of their room, the housekeeping team could be rewarded with a small celebration, like a cake from a local bakery. This not only shows appreciation but also reinforces the value of their hard work.

Engaging in fun, team-building activities can also enhance team spirit. A restaurant manager might organize a friendly cooking competition among the kitchen staff, with the winning dish featured as a special menu item for a week. This not only builds camaraderie but also encourages creativity and collaboration.

Simple gestures can make a big difference. For example, a silly sign on the bulletin board highlighting a team member's quirky talent can bring a smile to everyone's face and lighten the mood. A blue ribbon placed on a desk to recognize a job well done can serve as a visual reminder of appreciation and achievement.

Putting in a little effort to show you care about your team can lead to a significant return in cooperation and enthusiasm. When employees feel valued and part of a cohesive group, they are more likely to work together effectively, leading to better service and a more positive work environment.

In summary, developing and maintaining team spirit involves recognizing and celebrating immediate achievements, engaging in team-building activities, and showing genuine care through small, thoughtful gestures. This creates an environment where employees feel motivated, valued, and excited to contribute to the success of the team and the organization.

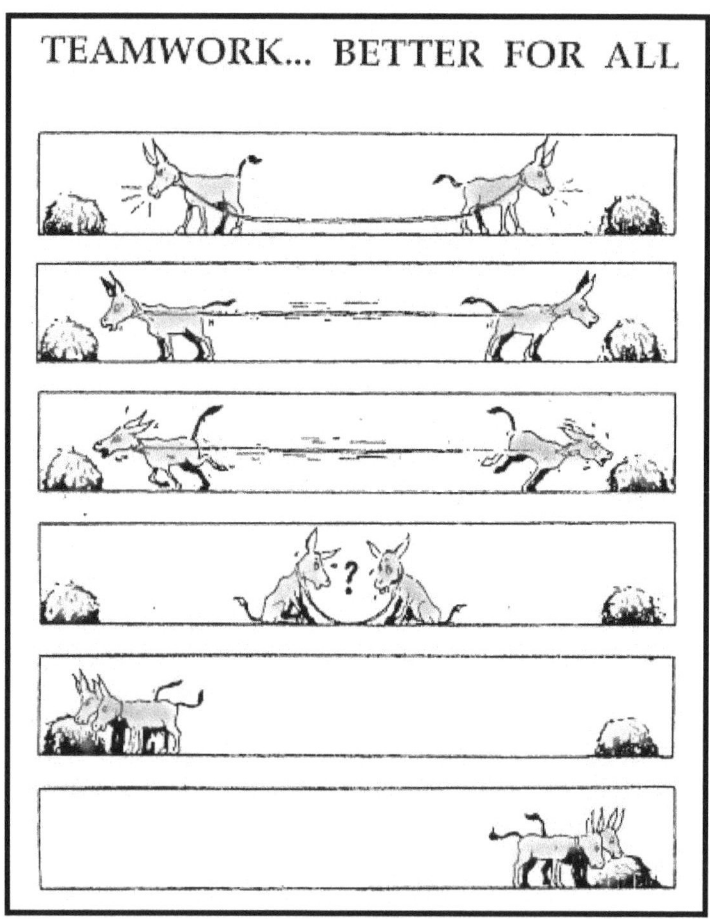

4. Share Your Knowledge: Teaching for Growth and Success

A good leader spends a lot of time teaching their team. In the hospitality industry, this is crucial, even though it might not seem immediately productive. It often feels quicker to do a task yourself than to explain how to do it to someone else. However, if you always do it yourself, you'll end up doing it over and over, rather than teaching someone else to handle it.

For example, a hotel manager might find it faster to handle guest complaints personally. But by taking the time to train the front desk staff on effective complaint resolution techniques, the manager ensures that the staff can manage these situations independently in the future. This not only frees up the manager's time but also empowers the staff to handle challenges confidently.

The best leaders invest time in developing their employees, sharing their knowledge and skills so others can advance too. Employees in a hotel or restaurant want to grow and improve in their roles. For instance, a chef should take time to teach junior cooks advanced cooking techniques and kitchen management skills. This helps them become better at their jobs and prepares them for potential promotions.

Employees look forward to growth opportunities and promotions. It's your job to support them. If you don't train them because you think they're too valuable in their current role or because you're afraid they might surpass you, you risk losing them anyway. For example, if a front desk manager doesn't train their staff to handle check-in procedures independently, those employees might feel stuck and seek opportunities elsewhere.

Remember, a leader who trains their replacement is the best candidate for promotion. In the hospitality industry, a banquet manager who trains an assistant to handle event planning and execution shows they are ready to take on larger responsibilities, potentially leading to a higher position within the company.

In summary, teaching what you know is essential for building a capable and motivated team. By investing time in training your employees, you help them grow, improve job satisfaction, and ensure the smooth operation of your department. This approach not only benefits the employees but also positions you as a forward-thinking leader ready for greater challenges and opportunities.

Share Your Knowledge

5. Record-Keeping Excellence: The Secret to Smooth Operations

In the hospitality industry, keeping accurate and detailed records is essential, whether you love paperwork or hate it. Understanding your preference can help you manage this crucial task effectively.

- **Delegate If You Dislike Paperwork**:

  If paperwork isn't your strong suit, delegate it to someone who excels in it. For example, a hotel manager who finds paperwork tedious can assign a detail-oriented administrative assistant to handle reports and records. This way, the manager can focus on overseeing guest services and staff management while ensuring all necessary documentation is maintained.

- **Supervise Delegated Tasks**:

  Even if you delegate, you must supervise and stay informed about what's happening. For instance, if you've delegated inventory management to a team member, regularly review the records to ensure supplies are tracked accurately and orders are placed on time. This helps in maintaining control over essential operations without getting bogged down by paperwork.

- **Provide Necessary Data for Others**:

  Keeping good records is vital for providing your boss and successors with the information they need. For example, detailed records of guest preferences, booking trends, and maintenance schedules can help the next manager continue providing excellent service without missing a beat. It ensures continuity and smooth transitions within the organization.

- **Limit Time Spent on Paperwork If You Enjoy It**:

  If you love paperwork, it's essential to discipline yourself to limit the time spent on it. Allocate specific times of the day for paperwork and dedicate the rest to interacting with staff and guests. For instance, a restaurant manager might set aside an hour each morning to handle paperwork and then spend the rest of the day on the floor, ensuring operations run smoothly and addressing any issues that arise.

- **Balance Desk Work and Field Work**:

  A good leader balances desk work with being present where the action is. For example, while it's crucial to maintain financial records, spending too much time at the desk can disconnect you from the day-to-day operations. By balancing office time with floor time, you stay engaged with both administrative duties and the practical aspects of running the business.

In summary, whether you love or hate paperwork, managing it effectively is crucial in the hospitality industry. Delegating tasks, supervising records, providing necessary data, and balancing your time between desk work and field work are key strategies. This approach ensures that you maintain accurate records without compromising your ability to lead and manage your team effectively.

Importance of Keeping Good Records in a Hospitality Organization

1. **Efficient Operations**:

   - Streamlines daily operations by tracking bookings, inventory, and staff schedules.
   - Ensures smooth check-ins and check-outs.

2. **Financial Management**:

   - Helps in monitoring expenses and revenues accurately.
   - Facilitates budgeting and financial planning.

3. **Customer Satisfaction**:

   - Maintains detailed guest preferences and feedback for personalized services.

 HOW TO BECOME A CELEBRITY LEADER IN HOSPITALITY INDUSTRY

- Enhances the guest experience by addressing their needs promptly.

4. **Compliance and Legal Protection**:

   - Ensures adherence to industry regulations and standards.

   - Provides evidence in case of disputes or audits.

5. **Employee Management**:

   - Tracks staff performance, attendance, and training records.

   - Aids in efficient workforce management and development.

6. **Inventory Control**:

   - Monitors stock levels to prevent shortages or overstocking.

   - Ensures availability of essential supplies and materials.

7. **Strategic Planning**:

   - Provides data for analysing trends and making informed decisions.

   - Assists in setting long-term goals and strategies for growth.

8. **Risk Management**:

   - Keeps records of incidents and maintenance to prevent future issues.

   - Enhances safety protocols and reduces liability risks.

I have noticed in different corporates the behaviour or the attitudes of the staff changes before their appraisal.

Suddenly they become very loyal towards their boss and they become extraordinarily efficient during this period.

Because they know, appraisal is approaching and they try their level best to make no stone unturned to please their boss.

I have seen during this period many leaders are emotionally trapped and they take decisions during the appraisal of their team members considering the present behaviour of these team members who are actually lazy and worthless during the whole year. This happens because, the so called leaders do not maintain the records of the performance of their team members.

That is the reason, I always suggest to maintain a good record for the performance of the team members throughout the year whenever they do a good job as well as they do a bad job. This will be the reference record for the leaders during the appraisal of their team members. This will give the proper justice to the team members who are really work hard and effective throughout the year.

1. Set a Good Example: "Don't Expect Them to Obey Rules if You Do Not"

a. Punctuality and Attendance:

- Example: If you expect your employees to be on time, make sure you arrive on time or earlier. A hotel manager who consistently arrives late to morning meetings will find it difficult to enforce punctuality among the staff.

b. Dress Code:

- Example: If your hotel has a strict dress code, adhere to it yourself. A restaurant manager who dresses casually while expecting staff to wear uniforms will undermine the dress code policy.

c. Professional Conduct:

- Example: Treat guests and employees with respect and courtesy at all times. If a manager is seen shouting at staff or guests, it sets a negative example and can lead to a toxic work environment.

d. Work Ethic:

- Example: Show dedication and a strong work ethic. A housekeeping supervisor who takes short-cuts or avoids difficult tasks sets a poor example for their team, who may then follow suit.

e. Adhering to Procedures:

- Example: Follow all hotel procedures and protocols, such as checking ID for guest check-ins. If a front desk manager skips these steps, employees may also neglect important security measures.

f. Maintaining Cleanliness:

- Example: Keep your workspace clean and organized. If the head chef maintains a messy workstation, kitchen staff may not see the importance of cleanliness, impacting overall hygiene standards.

g. Customer Service:

- Example: Provide excellent customer service. If the manager is seen going above and beyond for guests, such as helping with luggage or resolving issues promptly, employees will be inspired to do the same.

h. Compliance with Health and Safety Regulations:

- Example: Wear appropriate personal protective equipment (PPE) and follow health guidelines. A spa manager who neglects to wear a mask or sanitize equipment may find it challenging to enforce these rules among their team.

i. Communication:

- Example: Communicate clearly and effectively. If a banquet manager regularly updates their team and listens to their feedback, it sets a standard for open communication throughout the staff.

j. Continuing Education and Training:

- Example: Participate in training sessions and encourage staff to do the same. A hotel manager who actively engages in professional development demonstrates the importance of ongoing learning to their team.

By setting a good example in these areas, leaders in the hospitality industry can foster a positive work environment, ensure rules are followed, and ultimately provide better service to guests.

2. Treat Them as Individuals: "No Two People Are Alike

This concept means recognizing and valuing the unique qualities, strengths, and needs of each employee. Instead of applying a one-size-fits-all approach, leaders should understand that each person has different skills, preferences, and circumstances. By acknowledging these differences, leaders can create a more inclusive and effective work environment. This involves personalized training, flexible scheduling, tailored feedback, and individual career development plans. Ultimately, it's about showing respect for each person's individuality, leading to higher job satisfaction, better performance, and a more cohesive team.

a. Understanding Personal Strengths:

- Example: Recognize that some employees excel in customer interactions while others may be better suited for behind-the-scenes roles. A front desk agent who is naturally outgoing can thrive in welcoming guests, while a detail-oriented staff member might excel in managing reservations and billing.

b. Customized Training Programs:

- Example: Tailor training sessions to suit individual learning styles. For instance, a new server who learns best through hands-on experience should be paired with a seasoned mentor, while another who prefers reading might benefit more from detailed training manuals.

c. Flexible Scheduling:

- Example: Some employees may prefer working morning shifts while others might be night owls. By accommodating these preferences, such as allowing a chef who thrives in the evening to work dinner shifts, you can optimize performance and job satisfaction.

d. Personalized Feedback:

- Example: Give feedback in a way that resonates with each employee. A kitchen staff member who appreciates direct, straightforward comments should receive concise feedback, whereas a front desk clerk who is more sensitive might benefit from a more supportive and encouraging approach.

e. Career Development Plans:

- Example: Create individual career paths based on employees' goals and interests. If a housekeeper shows an interest in event planning, provide them with opportunities to assist in setting up conferences and meetings, gradually introducing them to a potential new role.

f. Cultural Sensitivity:

- Example: Acknowledge and respect the diverse cultural backgrounds of your team. During holiday seasons, for example, ensure that all cultural celebrations are acknowledged and respected, allowing a diverse team to feel included and valued.

g. Recognition and Rewards:

- Example: Tailor recognition and rewards to what each employee values most. Some might appreciate public acknowledgment in team meetings, while others might prefer a private note of thanks or a small bonus.

h. Work-Life Balance:

- Example: Be mindful of each employee's personal circumstances. An employee who is a single parent might need flexible hours or the ability to work from home occasionally, while another might appreciate the opportunity for overtime.

i. Conflict Resolution:

- Example: Address conflicts considering the personalities involved. A dispute between a quiet, reserved staff member and an outspoken colleague should be mediated differently, ensuring both feel heard and understood.

j. Health and Wellness Support:

- Example: Offer support programs that cater to different needs. For instance, a physically demanding role in the housekeeping department might require regular physiotherapy sessions, while a high-stress role in event management might benefit from mindfulness or stress management workshops.

By treating each employee as an individual and recognizing their unique strengths, preferences, and needs, leaders in the hospitality industry can create a more harmonious and productive work environment. This approach not only enhances job satisfaction and performance but also fosters a culture of respect and understanding.

Respect people not by boundaries but as human beings.
Don't go by human but by humanity.
Respect people's space
Respect people's priority
Treat others with dignity they deserve.

3. Be Fair, Never Play Favourites

Being fair and not playing favourites means treating all employees equally and justly, without giving preferential treatment to some over others. This practice is essential for maintaining trust, morale, and a positive work environment. In the hospitality industry, where teamwork and service quality are paramount, fairness ensures that every team member feels valued and motivated. Below are specific examples.

a. Equal Opportunities for Growth:

- Example: Ensure that all employees have access to training programs and career advancement opportunities. For instance, if you offer a training session on new reservation software, make sure all relevant staff members, not just your top performers, have the chance to attend.

b. Consistent Enforcement of Rules:

- Example: Apply hotel policies consistently to all employees. If a housekeeper is reprimanded for being late, the same standard should apply to the front desk manager. This consistency builds trust and respect among the team.

c. Objective Performance Reviews:

- Example: Use standardized criteria for performance evaluations. Instead of basing appraisals on personal feelings, rely on measurable outcomes like guest satisfaction scores or number of tasks completed on time. This approach ensures fairness in raises and promotions.

d. Fair Distribution of Shifts:

- Example: Rotate shifts and desirable assignments evenly. For instance, if working weekend shifts or high-tipping areas in a restaurant is considered advantageous, make sure these opportunities are distributed fairly among all staff, not just a select few.

e. Transparent Reward Systems:

- Example: Implement a clear and transparent system for bonuses and rewards. If you have a program that rewards staff for excellent guest feedback, ensure the criteria and process are known to everyone and that all have an equal chance to earn the rewards.

f. Listening to All Voices:

- Example: Encourage and value input from all team members, not just those you are closest to. In staff meetings, make it a point to ask for suggestions from everyone, including quieter members, to show that all opinions are valued.

g. Equal Access to Resources:

- Example: Provide equal access to tools and resources needed to perform their jobs. For example, ensure all housekeeping staff have the same quality cleaning supplies and equipment, and all kitchen staff have access to the same quality ingredients and tools.

h. Uniform Disciplinary Actions:

- Example: Handle disciplinary issues in the same manner for everyone. If two employees commit the same infraction, they should face the same consequences, regardless of their positions or personal relationships with management.

i. Balanced Workload Distribution:

- Example: Distribute tasks and responsibilities evenly among employees. Avoid overburdening reliable staff while underutilizing others. For instance, ensure that both experienced and newer team members share the workload during peak times.

j. Inclusive Recognition Programs:

- Example: Recognize and reward a variety of contributions, not just high-profile ones. Acknowledge behind-the-scenes efforts, such as a kitchen assistant's meticulous prep work, as well as front-of-house achievements, like a concierge's excellent guest service.

By adhering to the principle of fairness and avoiding favouritism, leaders in the hospitality industry can foster a positive and productive work environment. This approach not only boosts morale and teamwork but also enhances overall service quality, benefiting both employees and guests.

4. Inspire the Sense of Belongingness

Creating a sense of belonging among employees means fostering an environment where every team member feels valued, connected, and integral to the success of the organization. This sense of belonging boosts morale, enhances teamwork, and improves overall job satisfaction. In the hospitality industry, where employee engagement directly impacts guest experiences, inspiring a sense of belonging is crucial. Here are specific examples from the hospitality industry:

a. Inclusive Onboarding Process:

- Example: When new employees join a hotel, ensure they are warmly welcomed and introduced to all team members, not just their immediate co-workers. Provide a comprehensive orientation that includes a tour of the property, introductions to key staff members, and an overview of the hotel's culture and values.

b. Regular Team-Building Activities:

- Example: Organize regular team-building events, such as staff outings, workshops, or volunteer activities. For instance, a hotel might host a monthly team lunch or an annual picnic where employees from different departments can interact and bond in a relaxed setting.

c. Open Communication Channels:

- Example: Encourage open and transparent communication by holding regular staff meetings and creating platforms for employees to share their ideas and feedback. A suggestion box in the staff lounge or a digital forum where team members can voice their opinions can make everyone feel heard and valued.

d. Recognition Programs:

- Example: Implement a recognition program that celebrates employees' achievements and contributions. This could be an "Employee of the Month" award or a wall of fame in the staff area, highlighting individuals' efforts and accomplishments in front of their peers.

e. Personalized Support and Development:

- Example: Show genuine interest in employees' career aspirations and provide opportunities for professional growth. For example, if a concierge expresses interest in event planning, offer them cross-training opportunities in the events department to help them develop new skills.

f. Cultural Celebrations and Acknowledgment:

- Example: Celebrate cultural diversity by acknowledging and celebrating various cultural festivals and holidays. A hotel could host a potluck where employees bring dishes from their cultures, or decorate the staff areas to reflect different holidays celebrated by the team.

g. Employee Resource Groups (ERGs):

- Example: Establish ERGs focused on various interests or demographic groups within the hotel. These groups can provide support, foster connections, and offer a platform for employees to share their experiences. An ERG for sustainability enthusiasts could organize eco-friendly initiatives within the hotel.

h. Transparent Career Pathways:

- Example: Clearly outline potential career paths within the organization and provide resources for employees to advance. Offer mentorship programs where seasoned staff members guide newer employees, helping them navigate their career development within the hotel.

i. Employee Wellness Programs:

- Example: Implement wellness programs that address physical, mental, and emotional well-being. A hotel could offer yoga classes, stress management workshops, or provide access to counselling services, showing employees that their overall well-being is a priority.

j. Inclusive Decision-Making:

- Example: Involve employees in decision-making processes that affect their work and the hotel environment. For example, when planning a renovation of the staff break room, solicit input from employees about what improvements they would like to see, making them feel a part of the change.

By taking these steps, leaders in the hospitality industry can cultivate a strong sense of belonging among their employees. This not only enhances job satisfaction and retention but also translates into better service and a more welcoming atmosphere for guests.

5. Do Not Ration Information

Ensuring that employees have access to the information they need is crucial for their performance, morale, and engagement. Rationing information can lead to misunderstandings, decreased productivity, and a lack of trust. In the hospitality industry, where teamwork and effective communication are essential, sharing information openly can significantly enhance operations and guest satisfaction. Here are specific examples from the hospitality industry:

a. Transparent Communication:

- Example: Hold regular staff meetings where updates about the hotel's performance, upcoming events, and changes in policies are shared. This ensures that everyone is on the same page and can plan their work accordingly. For instance, if a major event is coming up, all departments should be informed in advance to prepare adequately.

b. Clear Job Expectations:

- Example: Provide detailed job descriptions and training manuals for all positions. For example, a new front desk agent should receive a comprehensive guide on check-in/check-out procedures, handling guest complaints, and using the reservation system. This clarity helps employees understand their roles and responsibilities fully.

c. Access to Performance Data:

- Example: Share performance metrics with the team. If a hotel tracks guest satisfaction scores, share these results with all staff members and discuss ways to improve. For instance, if the housekeeping team sees low scores in cleanliness, they can focus on addressing specific issues highlighted by guests.

d. Regular Feedback and Updates:

- Example: Provide regular feedback to employees about their performance and progress. For example, a chef should receive feedback on customer satisfaction with the dishes, helping them understand what's working well and what might need improvement.

e. Involve Employees in Decision-Making:

- Example: When making decisions that affect the team, involve employees in the process. If a hotel is considering changing its uniform policy, gather input from the staff who will be wearing the uniforms. This inclusion helps employees feel valued and more likely to support the final decision.

f. Training and Development Opportunities:

- Example: Ensure that all employees are aware of available training and development opportunities. For instance, if the hotel offers a customer service workshop, promote it across all departments so that anyone interested can participate.

g. Crisis Communication Plans:

- Example: In case of emergencies, have a clear communication plan in place. For example, during a fire drill or an actual emergency, ensure that all staff know the evacuation procedures and their roles. This preparedness can save lives and prevent chaos.

h. Project and Event Details:

- Example: Share detailed plans for upcoming projects or events. If the hotel is hosting a large wedding, ensure that all departments know the schedule, guest count, special requests, and any specific responsibilities. This coordination ensures smooth execution and enhances the guest experience.

i. Resource and Tool Availability:

- Example: Make sure employees know what resources and tools are available to them. For instance, if new software is introduced for booking management, provide training sessions and access to tutorials so that everyone can use it effectively.

j. Company Goals and Vision:

- Example: Regularly communicate the hotel's goals, vision, and values to all employees. This helps them understand the bigger picture and how their work contributes to the hotel's success. For example, if the hotel is aiming to achieve a specific sustainability certification, inform all staff about the initiatives and how they can contribute.

By ensuring that information flows freely and openly, leaders in the hospitality industry can foster a more informed, engaged, and productive workforce. This transparency builds trust, enhances teamwork, and ultimately leads to better service and higher guest satisfaction.

6. Deal with Rumours at Once

Rumours can quickly spread misinformation, lower morale, and create a toxic work environment if not addressed promptly. In the hospitality industry, where teamwork and a positive atmosphere are crucial for providing excellent guest experiences, it is vital to handle rumours effectively and swiftly. Here's how to deal with rumours in the hospitality industry with specific examples for employees:

a. Address Rumours Immediately:

- Example: If a rumour starts circulating that the hotel might be sold, address it immediately. Hold a staff meeting to clarify the situation. Provide factual information about the hotel's status and reassure employees about their job security, if applicable. Promptly dispelling the rumour prevents unnecessary anxiety and speculation.

b. Encourage Open Communication:

- Example: Create an environment where employees feel comfortable asking questions and raising concerns. For instance, set up regular Q&A sessions where staff can voice any rumours they've heard and receive accurate information in response. This openness reduces the spread of false information and promotes transparency.

c. Use Official Channels for Communication:

- Example: If a significant change is coming, such as a new management team or policy changes, announce it through official channels like staff meetings, emails, or the company intranet. For instance, if the hotel is changing its reservation system, send a detailed email explaining the reasons, the timeline, and how it will benefit both staff and guests. This ensures that everyone receives the same accurate information.

d. Investigate the Source of the Rumour:

- Example: If a rumour about changes in staff bonuses starts circulating, investigate where it originated. Talk to employees to understand their concerns and find the source. Address the root cause directly by clarifying the hotel's bonus policy and dispelling any misconceptions.

e. Provide Regular Updates:

- Example: Keep employees informed about ongoing projects or changes within the hotel. For instance, if there's a renovation happening, provide regular updates on the progress, any disruptions expected, and the benefits once completed. This proactive communication reduces the likelihood of rumours starting from uncertainty.

f. Foster a Culture of Trust:

- Example: Build a culture where trust is paramount. For instance, if an employee hears a rumour about reduced working hours, they should feel comfortable approaching their manager to verify the information. Managers should be approachable and willing to discuss and dispel any false information.

g. Educate Employees on the Impact of Rumours:

- Example: Conduct training sessions on the negative impact of rumours. Explain how rumours can harm teamwork, morale, and overall guest service. Use real-life scenarios or past incidents to illustrate these points. For example, discuss how a previous rumour about job cuts caused unnecessary panic and reduced staff productivity.

h. Lead by Example:

- Example: As a leader, demonstrate integrity and transparency in all communications. If you hear a rumour, address it openly and honestly with your team. For instance, if there's a rumour about a new dress code policy, clarify the truth and provide reasons for any actual changes, ensuring employees understand and accept them.

i. Encourage Reporting of Rumours:

- Example: Create a system where employees can report rumours confidentially. For instance, have an anonymous suggestion box or a designated HR contact. This allows management to address and investigate rumours before they escalate.

j. Highlight the Consequences of Spreading Rumours:

- Example: Make it clear that spreading false information is unacceptable. Set policies that outline the consequences of intentionally spreading rumours. For instance, include a section in the employee handbook that details disciplinary actions for spreading malicious rumours and emphasize the importance of maintaining a positive work environment.

By dealing with rumours swiftly and effectively, leaders in the hospitality industry can maintain a positive and productive work environment. This proactive approach ensures that employees remain focused, motivated, and aligned with the hotel's goals, ultimately leading to better guest experiences and overall success.

7. True Leadership is about Guidance, not Power Plays.

a. Balance Authority with Empathy

Meaning: Authority should be exercised with a sense of empathy and understanding rather than as a means to assert dominance.

Example: In a hotel setting, if a guest has a complaint, the front desk manager should address it with empathy and practical solutions rather than merely asserting their authority. They might listen to the guest's concerns and offer a resolution that shows understanding, rather than just enforcing hotel policies rigidly.

b. Lead by Example

Meaning: Demonstrate the behaviours and values you expect from your team through your actions rather than through commands.

Example: If a restaurant manager arrives on time, works diligently, and treats all staff with respect, they set a standard for the team. This approach is more effective than using their position to command punctuality or performance.

c. Encourage Team Autonomy

Meaning: Allow team members to make decisions and solve problems within their roles without constantly seeking managerial approval.

Example: A hotel housekeeping supervisor might empower staff to decide how to handle special guest requests (like extra amenities) rather than making every decision themselves. This builds trust and fosters a sense of responsibility among employees.

d. Foster Open Communication

Meaning: Create an environment where team members feel comfortable expressing their opinions and concerns, rather than feeling intimidated by authority.

Example: Instead of using authority to shut down feedback, a restaurant manager might hold regular meetings where staff can openly discuss issues and suggest improvements. This encourages a collaborative atmosphere and shows that their input is valued.

e. Use Authority to Support, Not Control

Meaning: Use your authority to provide resources, guidance, and support rather than to micromanage or enforce compliance.

Example: If a hotel team is struggling with a new booking system, a manager should offer additional training and resources rather than merely enforcing compliance with the system's use. This supportive approach helps the team adapt and perform better.

f. Build Trust Through Fairness

Meaning: Apply rules and policies consistently and fairly to build trust and respect among the team.

Example: A restaurant manager should enforce scheduling policies equally across all staff members, ensuring no favouritism. This fairness helps build trust and shows that authority is used to maintain standards, not to exert power.

g. Focus on Collaborative Leadership

Meaning: Engage with your team in decision-making and problem-solving rather than relying solely on top-down directives.

Example: When planning a new menu or service change, involve team members in brainstorming sessions and feedback discussions. This collaborative approach shows that their input is valued and reduces the need for authoritative decrees.

h. Address Issues Constructively

Meaning: Use authority to address problems constructively and helpfully rather than through punitive measures.

Example: If an employee repeatedly misses shifts, a manager should discuss the issue openly with the employee to understand any underlying problems and find a solution together, rather than issuing immediate disciplinary action.

Using authority in these ways helps to foster a positive work environment, build trust, and improve overall team morale.

8. Speak wisely—once words are out, they're hard to take back

In the hospitality industry, where effective communication is key to maintaining a positive work environment, choosing words carefully is essential. Here's a detailed breakdown of how this principle applies to interactions with employees

a. Think Before Speaking

Meaning: Consider the impact of your words before expressing them to avoid misunderstandings or unintended harm.

Example: A hotel manager should think carefully before addressing a staff member about performance issues. Instead of saying, "You're always late," which can sound accusatory, they might say, "I've noticed a few late arrivals and would like to discuss how we can ensure timely shifts."

b. Provide Constructive Feedback

Meaning: Use language that is supportive and aimed at helping employees improve rather than just criticizing.

Example: Instead of telling a restaurant server, "You messed up the order again," a manager might say, "I noticed there were some issues with the orders today. Let's review the process to see how we can avoid these mistakes in the future."

c. Avoid Public Criticism

Meaning: Deliver feedback or criticism privately to avoid embarrassing or demoralizing employees.

Example: If a housekeeping staff member has made an error, address it in a private meeting rather than in front of the team. For instance, rather than pointing out mistakes during a team meeting, discuss them in a one-on-one setting to respect the staff member's dignity.

d. Be Clear and Specific

Meaning: Use precise language to avoid confusion and ensure that your message is understood.

Example: When assigning tasks, a hotel supervisor should be specific about expectations. Instead of saying, "Make sure the rooms are ready," they could say, "Please ensure all guest rooms are cleaned, beds are made, and amenities are restocked by 3 PM."

e. Show Empathy and Respect

Meaning: Use language that shows understanding and respect for employees' feelings and perspectives.

Example: If an employee is dealing with a personal issue affecting their work, a compassionate approach would be, "I understand you're going through a tough time. How can we support you while you're managing this?" This approach demonstrates care and respect for their situation.

f. Avoid Overpromising

Meaning: Be realistic and honest about what you can deliver to maintain trust and credibility.

Example: Instead of promising a promotion or raise without confirming it, a manager might say, "I appreciate your hard work, and I will discuss your performance with senior management to explore potential opportunities."

g. Handle Conflict Calmly

Meaning: Address conflicts or disagreements with a calm and measured approach to avoid escalating the situation.

Example: If there's a dispute between team members, a manager should use neutral language like, "Let's discuss the issues and find a solution that works for both of you," rather than taking sides or using inflammatory language.

h. Encourage Open Communication

Meaning: Foster an environment where team members feel comfortable sharing their thoughts and feedback without fear of negative repercussions.

Example: A manager might say, "I value your feedback on how we can improve our service. Please feel free to share any suggestions or concerns you have." This encourages a culture of open dialogue and mutual respect.

9. Give Sincere & Honest Appreciation"

In the hospitality industry, genuine and heartfelt appreciation can significantly boost team morale and performance. Here's a detailed breakdown of how to offer sincere and honest appreciation to employees, with examples:

a. Recognize Specific Achievements

Meaning: Appreciate employees by acknowledging their specific contributions rather than giving generic praise.

Example: If a hotel receptionist goes above and beyond by handling a complex reservation issue with exceptional customer service, a manager might say, "I noticed how you efficiently resolved the guest's reservation issue today. Your attention to detail and patience made a big difference."

b. Be Timely with Your Praise

Meaning: Provide appreciation soon after the achievement to ensure it is relevant and meaningful.

Example: After a restaurant server receives positive feedback from a guest, the manager should promptly thank the server, saying, "I heard from a guest today that you provided outstanding service. I wanted to personally thank you for making their experience memorable."

c. Personalize Your Appreciation

Meaning: Tailor your praise to the individual's personal style and contributions to make it more meaningful.

Example: If a housekeeping staff member takes extra care in arranging special amenities for a guest, the supervisor might say, "I really appreciated the extra touch you added to the guest's room setup. Your thoughtfulness really stands out and enhances our guest experience."

d. Publicly Acknowledge Contributions

Meaning: Share appreciation with the team to highlight the individual's impact and inspire others.

Example: During a team meeting, a manager might say, "I want to give a shout out to our front desk team for their exceptional handling of the high guest volume this past weekend. Your hard work and dedication did not go unnoticed."

e. Offer Tangible Rewards

Meaning: Complement verbal praise with tangible rewards to show genuine appreciation.

Example: A restaurant might offer a "Server of the Month" award or a small gift card to a team member who has shown exceptional performance. This shows that their hard work is not only appreciated but also valued with a tangible token of thanks.

f. Provide Constructive Feedback Along with Praise

Meaning: Combine appreciation with constructive feedback to support continuous improvement.

Example: If a hotel staff member handles a challenging situation well, a manager might say, "You did a great job managing the guest's complaint. For future situations, consider also offering additional solutions to enhance their experience even more."

g. Show Genuine Interest

Meaning: Express appreciation in a way that reflects a genuine understanding and acknowledgment of the employee's efforts.

Example: If a chef creates a new, popular dish, the restaurant owner might say, "I really enjoyed the new dish you created; it's a hit with our guests. I'd love to hear more about your inspiration for it."

h. Follow Up on Appreciation

Meaning: Check in periodically to show ongoing recognition and support.

Example: After acknowledging a team member's great performance, a manager might follow up a few weeks later with, "I wanted to check in and see how you're doing. Your work has been fantastic, and I appreciate your continued effort and dedication."

Sincere and honest appreciation not only motivates employees but also fosters a positive and supportive work environment in the hospitality industry.

Please remember

Provide appreciation that is specific, immediate, sincere, and free from qualifiers like "BUT"

1. Specific

Meaning: Tailor your praise to clearly acknowledge what the employee did well, rather than giving vague compliments.

Example: Instead of saying, "Good job today," a hotel manager might say, "You did an excellent job resolving the guest's issue with the room assignment. Your quick thinking and clear communication turned a potentially frustrating situation into a positive experience for them."

2. Immediate

Meaning: Offer appreciation as soon as possible after the accomplishment to ensure the recognition is timely and relevant.

Example: After a restaurant server goes above and beyond to handle a difficult customer, the manager should immediately say, "I noticed how you handled that challenging situation with the guest. Your calm and professional approach was impressive. Thank you for managing it so well."

3. Sincere

Meaning: Make sure your appreciation is heartfelt and genuine, reflecting a true acknowledgment of the employee's efforts.

Example: If a hotel housekeeper takes extra care to arrange a special surprise for a returning guest, the supervisor might say, "I really appreciate how you went the extra mile to make the guest's stay special. Your attention to detail and care truly enhance our guest experience."

4. Don't Qualify Praise with "BUT"

Meaning: Avoid undermining your praise with a "but" that introduces criticism or a condition, which can diminish the impact of the appreciation.

Example: Instead of saying, "You did a great job on the banquet setup, but there were a few small issues," you should say, "You did a great job on the banquet setup. Everything was well-organized, and the guests were very pleased. Thank you for your hard work and attention to detail."

By focusing on these principles, appreciation becomes more impactful, motivating employees and reinforcing positive behaviours without introducing unnecessary qualifiers or conditions.

10. Develop A Sense Of Humour

In the hospitality industry, a sense of humour can greatly enhance the work environment and improve interactions with both guests and team members. Here's how developing a sense of humour can positively impact team dynamics and service, with examples:

a. Lighten the Mood During Busy Times

Meaning: Use humour to reduce stress and create a more relaxed atmosphere during peak periods.

Example: During a particularly busy brunch service at a restaurant, the manager might make a light-hearted joke about the team's ability to handle the rush, such as, "Looks like we're on a mission to break the world record for most coffee refills in an hour!" This can help lighten the mood and make the stress of a busy shift more manageable.

b. Build Team Cohesion

Meaning: Use humour to strengthen relationships and create a sense of camaraderie among team members.

Example: A hotel concierge might share a funny story about a previous guest's quirky request during a team meeting, fostering laughter and bonding among colleagues. This helps build a positive team dynamic and makes the workplace more enjoyable.

c. Improve Guest Interactions

Meaning: Employ humour to create a friendly and approachable atmosphere for guests.

Example: When checking in guests, a front desk clerk might use a humorous comment to ease any travel-related stress, such as, "Welcome to our hotel! If you need any help with the luggage or a recommendation for dinner, just let me know. We promise not to judge your choice of pineapple pizza!"

d. Diffuse Tense Situations

Meaning: Use humour to calmly address and de-escalate conflicts or stressful situations.

Example: If a guest is upset about a minor issue with their room, a hotel staff member might say, "I understand the room wasn't exactly as you expected. Think of it as a surprise plot twist in your stay! Let me fix this so the rest of your stay can be a smooth, predictable experience."

e. Make Training More Engaging

Meaning: Incorporate humour into training sessions to make them more engaging and memorable.

Example: During a staff training session on handling difficult guests, the trainer might include humorous anecdotes about common guest behaviours, such as, "You might encounter guests who think they're the first to request an extra pillow. Just remember, you're not alone—every hotel has its pillow enthusiasts!"

f. Enhance Guest Experience

Meaning: Use humour to create memorable and enjoyable experiences for guests, adding to their overall satisfaction.

Example: At a resort, a bartender might use playful banter with guests while preparing drinks, such as, "If this margarita doesn't make your day better, I'm afraid nothing will. But I'm willing to keep trying until it does!"

g. Foster a Positive Work Environment

Meaning: Create a workplace where humour is used to uplift spirits and foster a positive atmosphere.

Example: During daily briefings, a manager might include a humorous comment or light-hearted joke to start the day on a positive note, such as, "Let's make today great, or at least better than last Monday's coffee!" This can help improve overall morale and create a more enjoyable work environment.

h. Handle Mistakes Gracefully

Meaning: Use humour to address mistakes in a way that minimizes embarrassment and promotes a learning environment.

Example: If a server accidentally spills a drink, they might say, "Well, I guess that's one way to give our guests a splash of excitement! Let me get you a fresh drink right away."

Developing a sense of humour in the hospitality industry can lead to a more pleasant work environment, better guest interactions, and a more cohesive and motivated team.

  HOW TO BECOME A CELEBRITY LEADER IN HOSPITALITY INDUSTRY

11. Avoid Sarcasm

In the hospitality industry, clear and respectful communication is crucial for maintaining a positive work environment and ensuring high-quality guest service. Here's how avoiding sarcasm benefits interactions with team members,

a. Promote Clear Communication

Meaning: Use straightforward language to avoid misunderstandings that sarcasm can cause.

Example: Instead of saying to a team member who is running late, "Oh great, just what we needed, another late start!" a manager should say, "I noticed you're running late. Is there anything I can do to help you manage your schedule better?"

b. Build Trust and Respect

Meaning: Avoid sarcasm to foster a respectful and supportive atmosphere where team members feel valued.

Example: When a server makes a mistake, instead of sarcastically saying, "Nice job messing up the order again," a manager should say, "I see there was an issue with the order. Let's go over what happened and how we can prevent it in the future."

c. Enhance Team Morale

Meaning: Avoiding sarcasm helps maintain high morale by ensuring that feedback is constructive and not demeaning.

Example: If a team member is struggling with a new procedure, rather than using sarcastic remarks like, "Looks like someone forgot to read the manual," a supervisor should offer support, saying, "I understand this new procedure can be tricky. Let's go through it together to make sure you're comfortable with it."

d. Ensure Positive Guest Interactions

Meaning: Maintain professionalism and positive interactions with guests by avoiding sarcastic comments.

Example: If a guest makes a special request, rather than saying, "Oh sure, because we have nothing better to do," a staff member should respond positively, "I'd be happy to help with that request. Let me see what I can do for you."

e. Model Professional Behaviour

Meaning: Demonstrate professionalism by avoiding sarcasm, setting a positive example for the team.

Example: During a staff meeting, instead of making sarcastic comments about a team member's performance, a leader should offer constructive feedback and encouragement, such as, "I appreciate your efforts in this area. Let's work on this specific point to help improve our overall performance."

f. Prevent Conflict and Misunderstandings

Meaning: Avoid sarcasm to reduce the risk of conflicts and ensure clear understanding among team members.

Example: If a team member is late to a shift, instead of sarcastically saying, "Well, it's not like we have a schedule or anything," a manager should say, "We need to stick to the schedule to ensure smooth operations. Can we discuss any challenges you're facing with timely arrivals?"

g. Encourage Open Dialogue

Meaning: Use direct communication to encourage open and honest conversations, fostering a supportive environment.

Example: When providing feedback on a task, rather than using sarcasm like, "Looks like you've really mastered this," say, "I noticed you're still working on this task. Let's review it together and see how we can make it more efficient."

h. Foster a Supportive Work Environment

Meaning: Avoid sarcasm to create a supportive and inclusive work environment where team members feel comfortable and motivated.

Example: If an employee is new and makes a mistake, rather than saying, "Well, that's a rookie mistake," provide supportive feedback like, "Everyone makes mistakes when they're new. Let's review what happened and go over how to handle it differently next time."

Avoiding sarcasm helps maintain a positive, respectful, and professional atmosphere in the hospitality industry, ensuring effective communication and enhancing team cohesion and guest satisfaction.

12. Practice Humility

In the hospitality industry, practicing humility involves recognizing and appreciating the contributions of others, staying grounded despite success, and being open to learning and growth. Here's how practicing humility benefits interactions with team members,

a. Acknowledge Team Contributions

Meaning: Recognize and credit the efforts of the entire team rather than taking all the credit yourself.

Example: After a successful event, a hotel manager might say, "The event went smoothly thanks to everyone's hard work and dedication. I appreciate all your efforts in making it a success." This acknowledges the collective effort rather than just the manager's leadership.

b. Be Open to Feedback

Meaning: Show willingness to listen to and act on feedback from team members, regardless of your position.

Example: If a restaurant manager receives suggestions from staff on improving service procedures, they might say, "Thank you for your feedback. I'll consider your ideas and see how we can implement them to improve our service.

c. Admit Mistakes

Meaning: Accept responsibility for errors and work to correct them, rather than shifting blame or making excuses.

Example: If a hotel manager made a scheduling error that affected staff shifts, they should say, "I apologize for the mix-up with the schedule. I'll correct it immediately and ensure it doesn't happen again.

d. Show Respect for All Roles

Meaning: Treat every team member with respect, regardless of their role or position within the organization.

Example: During a busy shift, a restaurant chef might thank the dishwasher by saying, "I appreciate your hard work tonight. The kitchen runs smoothly because of your efforts." This shows respect for all roles in the team.

e. Be Willing to Learn

Meaning: Approach every situation with a willingness to learn and improve, regardless of your level of experience.

Example: A senior hotel executive might attend a training session alongside new employees, showing that they value learning and growth, and saying, "I'm here to learn just as much as everyone else. We can all benefit from new perspectives.

f. Avoid Arrogance

Meaning: Stay grounded and avoid displaying arrogance or superiority, even if you've achieved significant success.

Example: After a successful guest review, instead of saying, "Our team's success is entirely due to my leadership," a manager might say, "I'm proud of what we've accomplished together. It's a team effort, and I'm grateful for everyone's hard work."

g. Offer Help and Support

Meaning: Be available to assist and support team members, showing that you value their needs and contributions.

Example: If a new team member is struggling with their tasks, a senior staff member might offer to help, saying, "I know this can be challenging at first. Let me show you a few tips that might make things easier."

h. Celebrate Others' Successes

Meaning: Celebrate and support the achievements of others, rather than focusing solely on your own successes.

Example: If a colleague receives an award for exceptional service, a manager might congratulate them by saying, "Congratulations on your award! Your dedication and hard work are truly inspiring to the whole team."

Practicing humility in the hospitality industry helps build a supportive and collaborative work environment, fosters respect among team members, and enhances overall team effectiveness and morale.

13

The Hallmarks of Leadership Excellence

Before going through this chapter, I will request you, please read chapter 3 once again

"Three Focus Point to Become Celebrity Leader"

You will be able to relate the content of this chapter and how you can achieve these flawlessly.

1. Loyal

a) Meaning: Loyalty involves showing consistent support and commitment to your team and organization.

b) Importance: Loyalty fosters trust and reliability within the team. A loyal leader earns the respect of their employees and cultivates a culture of dedication and mutual support.

A hotel manager who stands by their staff during difficult times, such as supporting them through personal issues or advocating for better working conditions, demonstrates loyalty. This commitment encourages employees to remain dedicated to the hotel and perform their best.

Loyalty is like money or affection: if you want to get it, you have to invest some of your own.

Don't criticize the company to your employees. To them, you represent the company.

Likewise, don't speak poorly of your employees to the company. If you expect them to perform well when you need them, you must treat them with respect and support.

2. Optimist

a) Meaning: An optimist maintains a positive and hopeful attitude, even in challenging situations.

b) Importance: Optimism motivates and inspires the team, helping to maintain morale and drive during tough times. An optimistic leader can see opportunities in challenges and encourage the team to strive for better outcomes.

During a downturn in tourism, an optimistic hotel manager might rally the team by highlighting potential opportunities for improvement and growth, such as offering new services or packages to attract local guests, rather than focusing on the negative aspects.

The optimist eagerly listens to others because he expects good news. The pessimist listens as little as possible because he expects bad news.

The optimist believes people are helpful, creative, and productive. The pessimist thinks they are lazy, resentful, and wasteful. Interestingly, both beliefs tend to become true.

The optimist starts each day with eagerness and confidence. The pessimist would rather stay in bed.

The optimist values the ideas of his team. The pessimist sees new ideas as problems that probably won't work.

As a result, the optimist tends to advance in the company, while the pessimist stays in the same position.

Do you know who Pessimists are ? They are

Unhappy – When there is no trouble
Feel Bad – When they feel good

Spend most time – In complaint counter
Turn off light – To see the darkness
Do not see the doughnut – But only the hole
Believe Sun shine – To cast shadow

3. Likes People

a) Meaning: A leader who likes people enjoys interacting with and understands the value of building strong relationships.

b) Importance: This quality helps in creating a welcoming and inclusive work environment. Leaders who genuinely like people can foster teamwork and collaboration more effectively.

A restaurant manager who takes the time to get to know each staff member, remembers personal details about them, and engages in friendly conversations shows that they value their team. This creates a positive and cohesive work atmosphere.

4. Courageous

a). Meaning: Courage involves taking risks and standing up for what is right, even in the face of adversity.

b) Importance: Courageous leaders can drive change and innovation. They are not afraid to make difficult decisions or defend their team when necessary, which can lead to significant improvements and a strong sense of trust.

A hotel manager who implements new eco-friendly practices despite initial resistance from stakeholders shows courage. By advocating for sustainable practices, they demonstrate a commitment to long-term benefits and ethical responsibility.

5. Looks Over the Fence

a) Meaning: This means having a forward-thinking mindset and being aware of trends and changes beyond the immediate environment.

b) Importance: Leaders who look over the fence can anticipate future challenges and opportunities, positioning their organization for long-term success.

Never say "it's not my job"

A hotel general manager who stays updated with industry trends, such as the growing demand for personalized guest experiences, and incorporates these trends into the hotel's services, ensures the business remains competitive and innovative.

6. Decisive

a) Meaning: Being decisive involves making clear, timely decisions and taking responsibility for their outcomes.

b) Importance: Decisive leaders provide direction and confidence to their team. They help avoid delays and uncertainty, which can be detrimental in a fast-paced industry like hospitality.

A restaurant manager who quickly decides to implement a new menu item based on customer feedback and market research demonstrates decisiveness. This prompt action can enhance the dining experience and attract more guests.

7. Tactful & Considerate

a) Meaning: Tactful and considerate leaders handle situations delicately and respectfully, being mindful of others' feelings and perspectives.

b) Importance: This quality helps in resolving conflicts smoothly and maintaining a harmonious work environment. It also fosters respect and trust among team members.

If a conflict arises between kitchen staff and servers, a tactful restaurant manager would address the issue privately and sensitively, ensuring both sides feel heard and working towards a mutually acceptable solution.

Please Remember

- You get more with honey than vinegar
- Consider others view/problem
- Don't ignore suggestions
- Allow others to save face
- Make every criticism a sandwich with a bread of praise.

8. Ambitious

a) Meaning: Ambition involves having a strong desire for success and continuous improvement.

b) Importance: Ambitious leaders drive growth and innovation. Their enthusiasm and vision can motivate the entire team to strive for higher standards and achieve significant goals.

A hotel manager who sets ambitious targets for customer satisfaction and strives to achieve a top rating on review platforms like TripAdvisor shows ambition. This not only enhances the hotel's reputation but also motivates the staff to deliver exceptional service.

9. Humble

a) Meaning: Humility involves recognizing your limitations, valuing others' contributions, and being open to feedback and learning.

b) Importance: Humble leaders create an environment where team members feel valued and encouraged to share ideas. This fosters collaboration and continuous improvement.

A hotel general manager who credits the entire team for a successful event and acknowledges their efforts publicly shows humility. This builds team morale and loyalty.

10. Self-Confident

a) Meaning: Self-confidence involves having a strong belief in your abilities and decisions.

b) Importance: Self-confident leaders inspire trust and confidence in their team. They can effectively lead and make decisions, even under pressure.

A confident hotel manager who calmly addresses a sudden crisis, such as an overbooking situation, and provides clear guidance on how to resolve it, reassures the team and ensures a smooth resolution.

Leaders Relies On Systems Only
Celebrity Leaders Relies On People

Sixer Action Tips to Become a Celebrity Leader

1. Become a People Watcher

a) Meaning: Observe and understand the behaviours, preferences, and needs of your team members.

b) Importance: This helps leaders build strong connections and tailor their approach to individual team members, fostering a supportive work environment.

In a busy hotel lobby, a manager might notice that a particular staff member excels in interacting with guests. By recognizing this, the manager can assign this employee to front desk duties, where their strengths can shine, improving guest satisfaction.

2. Send Out Inviting Vibes

a) Meaning: Create a welcoming and approachable atmosphere that encourages open communication.

b) Importance: Inviting vibes make employees feel comfortable sharing ideas and concerns, leading to better teamwork and innovation.

A restaurant manager who greets each team member with a smile and takes time to listen to their suggestions creates an environment where staff feel valued and motivated to contribute positively to the restaurant's success.

3. Be Cordial

a) Meaning: Display warmth and friendliness in all interactions with your team.

b) Importance: Cordiality fosters a positive work environment, reducing stress and increasing job satisfaction among employees.

A cordial hotel supervisor who consistently thanks housekeepers for their hard work and remembers their names builds a sense of community and appreciation, encouraging employees to maintain high standards of cleanliness and service.

4. Boost an Ego

a) Meaning: Offer genuine praise and recognition to uplift your team members' confidence and morale.

b) Importance: Boosting an ego can enhance performance and job satisfaction, as employees feel valued and acknowledged for their efforts.

When a chef creates a new dish that receives positive guest feedback, the restaurant owner publicly praises the chef's creativity and hard work during a staff meeting. This recognition boosts the chef's confidence and inspires others to innovate.

5. Admit Your Mistake

a) Meaning: Acknowledge and take responsibility for your errors.

b) Importance: Admitting mistakes demonstrates integrity and builds trust, showing employees that it's okay to be human and learn from errors.

If a hotel manager makes a scheduling error that affects staff shifts, admitting the mistake and working to correct it shows accountability and respect for the team. This honesty encourages a culture of transparency and mutual trust.

6. Visit Your Team

a) Meaning: Regularly spend time with your team in their working environment.

b) Importance: Visiting your team shows that you care about their work and are involved in the day-to-day operations, fostering a sense of solidarity and support.

A general manager who periodically joins the housekeeping team during their rounds or helps serve during peak hours in the restaurant demonstrates genuine interest in their team's experiences. This presence boosts morale and shows that the leader is part of the team, not just an overseer.

1. Begin with a Praise & Honest Appreciation

a) Meaning: Start any interaction with positive feedback and genuine recognition of the person's strengths or achievements.

b) Importance: This sets a positive tone for the conversation and helps the person feel valued and respected, making them more receptive to any subsequent feedback.

In a hotel setting, a manager might begin a conversation with a front desk employee by complimenting their excellent customer service skills before discussing areas for improvement in managing reservations.

2. Call Attention to People's Mistakes Indirectly

a) Meaning: Instead of pointing out mistakes directly, use a more subtle approach to highlight areas that need improvement.

b) Importance: This approach reduces defensiveness and helps maintain the person's dignity, leading to a more constructive and positive outcome.

A restaurant manager could use this approach by saying, "I've noticed our guests appreciate when their orders are confirmed before placing them. It helps avoid any confusion," rather than directly criticizing a server for making errors.

3. Talk About Your Own Mistakes Before Criticizing Others

a) Meaning: Share your own experiences of making similar mistakes before addressing someone else's errors.

b) Importance: This shows humility and relatability, making it easier for others to accept feedback and learn from it.

A hotel supervisor might say, "I remember when I first started, I also struggled with managing multiple tasks at once. Here are some strategies that helped me," before advising a new employee on time management.

4. Ask Questions Instead of Giving Direct Orders

a) Meaning: Frame directives as questions to involve the person in the decision-making process.

b) Importance: This encourages collaboration and empowers employees to think critically and take ownership of their actions.

A hotel manager could ask, "How do you think we can improve our check-in process to make it more efficient?" rather than giving a direct order to change the process. Guide them to think critically whenever necessary.

5. Let the Other Person Save Face

a) Meaning: Allow the person to maintain their dignity and self-respect during conversations about their mistakes or areas of improvement.

b) Importance: This helps preserve their confidence and motivation, ensuring they remain productive and positive. Never make fun out of someone's mistake. Never encourage gossip about someone's mistake with other team members.

If a housekeeper makes a mistake, a hotel manager might say, "I understand it's easy to miss details when things are busy. Let's work together to find a way to manage the workload more effectively," instead of harshly reprimanding them.

6. Praise in Public, Scold in Private

a) Meaning: Give praise and recognition in front of others, but address mistakes or criticisms privately.

b) Importance: Public praise boosts morale and motivates the team, while private criticism maintains individual dignity and prevents embarrassment.

A general manager could publicly commend a chef for their innovative dish during a team meeting but address any issues with food preparation in a private one-on-one conversation.

7. Give the Other Person a Fine Reputation to Live Up To

a) Meaning: Highlight the positive qualities and potential of the person, encouraging them to live up to that reputation.

b) Importance: This motivates individuals to meet the high expectations set for them, fostering personal and professional growth.

A hotel manager might tell a concierge, "You have a great reputation for handling guest requests efficiently. I have no doubt you'll manage this VIP guest's needs perfectly," boosting their confidence and performance.

8. Use Encouragement & Help to Correct Fault

a) Meaning: Offer support and guidance to help someone improve, rather than just pointing out what they did wrong.

b) Importance: Encouragement fosters a positive learning environment and helps build the person's skills and confidence.

If a server struggles with taking orders accurately, a restaurant manager could offer additional training sessions and encouragement, saying, "I know you can get the hang of this with a bit more practice. Let's go over the menu together."

9. Make the Other Person Happy About Doing the Thing You Want

a) Meaning: Present tasks or changes in a way that aligns with the person's interests and motivations.

b) Importance: This increases their willingness to comply and perform well, as they see the value and benefit in what they're being asked to do.

A hotel manager might motivate a team member by saying, "Your creativity would be perfect for designing our new guest welcome packages. It would really enhance our guests' experience and showcase your talent," making the task appealing and engaging.

1. Become genuinely interested in other people

Show a sincere interest in your team members' lives, both professionally and personally. A hotel manager might take the time to ask a front desk employee about their weekend or their hobbies. This shows that the manager values them as individuals and not just as workers.

A restaurant manager could ask a chef about their culinary background and what dishes they love to create, showing genuine interest in their professional journey. Additionally, a spa director might learn about a therapist's favourite wellness practices, making them feel seen and appreciated for their unique contributions.

2. SMILE – it takes 72 muscles to frown & only 14 to smile

A genuine smile can create a positive and welcoming environment. A restaurant manager who consistently smiles and maintains a cheerful demeanour will likely inspire the same behaviour in their staff, leading to a more pleasant atmosphere for both employees and guests.

A concierge who smiles warmly when greeting guests helps to create a welcoming first impression, encouraging guests to feel comfortable and valued. Similarly, a housekeeping supervisor who smiles and maintains a positive attitude can uplift their team, making their work environment more enjoyable and productive.

3. Call by name – the sweetest music to an individual

Addressing team members by their names fosters a sense of recognition and respect. A hotel supervisor makes it a point to greet each housekeeper by name during morning briefings, reinforcing their importance within the team.

A restaurant manager who thanks each server by name at the end of a busy shift reinforces their individual contributions to the team's success. In a spa, the director might personally acknowledge each therapist's efforts by name during team meetings, creating a stronger sense of individual value and team cohesion.

4. Encourage others to talk about themselves

Give your team members the opportunity to share their thoughts, ideas, and experiences. A restaurant manager might hold regular team meetings where servers are encouraged to discuss their experiences and suggest improvements, making them feel heard and valued.

A hotel manager could organize informal coffee breaks where team members can share their personal interests and hobbies, fostering a sense of community. Additionally, a spa manager might have one-on-one check-ins with therapists, encouraging them to discuss their professional goals and any challenges they face.

5. Talk in terms of other person's interest

Frame conversations around what matters to the team member to show you understand and care about their interests. A hotel manager discussing shift changes might focus on how the new schedule could benefit an employee's work-life balance, demonstrating empathy and consideration.

A restaurant manager might discuss a new menu item by relating it to a chef's culinary passions, showing appreciation for their expertise and creativity. Similarly, a hotel supervisor could talk about professional development opportunities in terms of an employee's career aspirations, aligning their work with their personal goals.

6. Make the other person feel important

Recognize and affirm the contributions and worth of each team member. A restaurant manager might publicly acknowledge a server's exceptional performance during a busy shift, making them feel appreciated and important to the team's success.

A hotel manager could highlight a front desk employee's outstanding customer service in a team meeting, reinforcing their value to the team. In a spa, the director might celebrate a therapist's innovative approach to treatments, emphasizing how their unique skills enhance the spa's offerings.

7. Have a big dose of patience, few drops of humility & a dash of humour & you will be rewarded in many fold

Cultivate patience, humility, and a sense of humour to build strong, positive relationships. A hotel supervisor dealing with a new employee's repeated mistakes might patiently explain the correct procedures, share a personal story about their own early mistakes, and lighten the mood with a joke to ease tension. This approach not only corrects the issue but also builds a supportive and enjoyable work environment.

A restaurant manager might handle a busy, stressful night by maintaining patience and using humour to keep the team's spirits high, showing that challenges can be managed with a positive attitude. Similarly, a spa manager could address a scheduling error with humility, admitting their own part in the mistake and using humour to diffuse any frustration, fostering a collaborative and forgiving team environment.

Six Deadly Mistakes Leaders Make with Their Teams

1. Doing things more to be liked than to be respected

When leaders prioritize being liked over being respected, they often compromise on rules and standards, which can undermine their authority and effectiveness. A hotel manager who constantly tries to please staff by overlooking policy violations, like tardiness or improper uniform, can lose respect over time. Staff may start to see the manager as lenient and unprofessional, leading to decreased discipline and performance.

A restaurant manager who gives in to all employee requests for schedule changes without considering the impact on the team can create chaos. While trying to be liked, they might end up being perceived as unable to maintain structure and fairness.

A spa director who allows employees to skip training sessions to avoid conflict can end up with a poorly trained team. This can result in lower service quality and ultimately diminish the director's credibility and authority.

2. Failing to ask for suggestions

Leaders who don't seek input from their team miss out on valuable insights and ideas, which can lead to poor decision-making and lower team morale. A hotel manager who implements new policies without seeking input from the front desk staff might miss out on practical insights. This could lead to inefficiencies or employee dissatisfaction as they feel their expertise is undervalued.

A restaurant manager who plans a new menu without consulting the chefs might overlook valuable suggestions that could enhance the offerings. This could result in lower team morale and missed opportunities for innovation.

A housekeeping supervisor who changes cleaning protocols without asking the team for feedback might face resistance. Employees who feel their experience and ideas are ignored may become disengaged and less motivated.

3. Failing to develop a sense of responsibility

When leaders don't encourage responsibility in their team, employees may not develop critical problem-solving skills or initiative. A hotel supervisor who micromanages every task can prevent team members from developing their own problem-solving skills. Employees might become overly reliant on the supervisor and less confident in their abilities.

A restaurant manager who never delegates important tasks to the team misses opportunities for employees to grow and take ownership. This can lead to a lack of initiative and lower job satisfaction among staff.

A spa manager who handles all client complaints personally without involving the team might hinder staff from learning how to manage difficult situations. This can result in a team that is unprepared to handle challenges independently.

4. Failure to keep your subordinate informed

Not keeping team members informed about changes and decisions can lead to confusion and inefficiency. A hotel manager who makes changes to guest check-in procedures without informing the front desk staff can create confusion and frustration. Staff may feel blindsided and unprepared to address guest concerns.

A restaurant manager who updates the menu without notifying servers can lead to service mishaps and guest dissatisfaction. Servers might feel embarrassed and unsupported when they are unaware of menu changes.

A housekeeping supervisor who schedules maintenance without informing the team can cause disruptions. Housekeepers might waste time or face difficulties completing their tasks efficiently due to unexpected changes.

5. Failure to keep criticism constructive

Negative feedback that is not constructive can demotivate employees and harm their confidence. A hotel manager who harshly criticizes a front desk employee for a mistake in front of guests can damage the employee's confidence and morale. Constructive feedback provided privately would be more effective and respectful.

A restaurant manager who angrily points out a server's error during a busy shift can create a stressful and hostile work environment. Offering constructive criticism after the shift in a calm manner would be more productive.

A spa manager who focuses solely on what a therapist did wrong without acknowledging their strengths can demotivate the employee. Balancing feedback with positive reinforcement helps maintain morale and encourages improvement.

6. Failure to solve problems & complaints

Ignoring or inadequately addressing problems and complaints can lead to persistent issues and lower team morale. A hotel manager who ignores repeated complaints about malfunctioning equipment can frustrate staff and hinder their ability to provide excellent service. Addressing issues promptly shows respect for the team's needs and supports their performance.

A restaurant manager who dismisses concerns about scheduling conflicts can create ongoing tension and dissatisfaction among staff. Actively seeking solutions and showing empathy can foster a more collaborative and harmonious work environment.

A spa director who fails to resolve conflicts between team members can lead to a toxic work atmosphere. Taking the time to mediate and find resolutions demonstrates commitment to a healthy, productive workplace.

Win Every Day with Six Powerful Words

SIX most important words

I ADMIT I MADE A MISTAKE

FIVE most important words

YOU DID A GOOD JOB

FOUR most important words

WHAT IS YOUR OPINION?

THREE most important words

IF YOU PLEASE

TWO most important words

THANK YOU

ONE most important word

WE

The LEAST important word

I

When 'i ' is
replaced By 'we'

Even
'illness'
Becomes
'Wellness'

Stay in the Game: Winners Never Quit

The hospitality industry is one of the most demanding fields, where staying strong and committed is crucial for success. The phrase "Stay in the Game: Winners Never Quit" perfectly captures what it takes to succeed in an industry filled with both challenges and opportunities. Let's explore this idea with simple examples from the hospitality world, showing how persistence can turn difficulties into achievements.

The Challenges of the Hospitality Industry

Working in the hospitality industry can be tough. Businesses face high expectations from customers, and they must quickly adapt to keep up with changing trends. The work is often stressful, with long hours and a constant need to provide excellent service. However, for those who don't give up, the industry also offers many opportunities to succeed.

The Story of Conrad Hilton

One of the best examples of not giving up in the hospitality industry is Conrad Hilton, the founder of Hilton Hotels. Hilton's path to building one of the world's largest hotel chains was filled with challenges. He faced many obstacles, including the Great Depression, which almost ruined his business. But Hilton didn't give up. He believed in his dream of creating a global hotel chain and kept pushing forward, even when things were difficult. Today, Hilton Hotels is a global name known for luxury and quality, thanks to his determination.

 HOW TO BECOME A CELEBRITY LEADER IN HOSPITALITY INDUSTRY

Overcoming Problems: The Case of Ritz-Carlton

Ritz-Carlton is another example of how not giving up can lead to success. In the 1990s, the brand faced criticism for inconsistent service across its hotels. Instead of quitting, Ritz-Carlton worked harder to improve. The company invested in training its staff and developed a unified service philosophy called "The Ritz-Carlton Gold Standards." This commitment to improvement not only saved the brand but also made it one of the most respected names in luxury hospitality.

Adapting and Succeeding: Marriott International

Marriott International, one of the largest hospitality companies in the world, shows how persistence can lead to success. Marriott started as a small root beer stand in Washington, D.C., and grew into a global hospitality leader. The company faced many challenges, including economic downturns and changes in customer preferences. But Marriott's leaders never gave up. By adapting to changing conditions and focusing on customer satisfaction, Marriott became a leader in the global hospitality market.

The Power of a Winning Attitude

What do these examples have in common? They all show the importance of having a winning attitude in the hospitality industry. Leaders like Conrad Hilton, the team at Ritz-Carlton, and the executives at Marriott International believe that quitting is not an option. They know that challenges are part of the journey, but they also know that staying persistent, being innovative, and committing to excellence are what make winners.

Lessons for Hospitality Leaders

For those working in the hospitality industry, these stories offer important lessons:

1. Stay Resilient: Being able to recover from setbacks is key. Whether it's a slow business period, a difficult customer, or an economic downturn, staying focused on your long-term goals is essential.

2. Keep Improving: The best hospitality brands always look for ways to get better. By refining processes, investing in staff training, and understanding customer needs, you can build a brand that lasts.

3. Be Adaptable: The hospitality industry is always changing. Winners are those who can adapt to new trends, technologies, and customer expectations while staying true to their values.

4. Never Lose Sight of Your Vision: Like Conrad Hilton, successful leaders keep their vision in mind, no matter how hard the journey gets. This long-term focus helps them overcome short-term challenges without losing direction.

Conclusion

The hospitality industry is challenging but rewarding. Those who succeed are the ones who live by the principle of "Stay in the Game: Winners Never Quit." By staying resilient, adaptable, and committed to continuous improvement, hospitality professionals can overcome obstacles and achieve lasting success. The stories of Hilton, Ritz-Carlton, and Marriott remind us that in this industry, winners are those who refuse to quit.

 HOW TO BECOME A CELEBRITY LEADER IN HOSPITALITY INDUSTRY

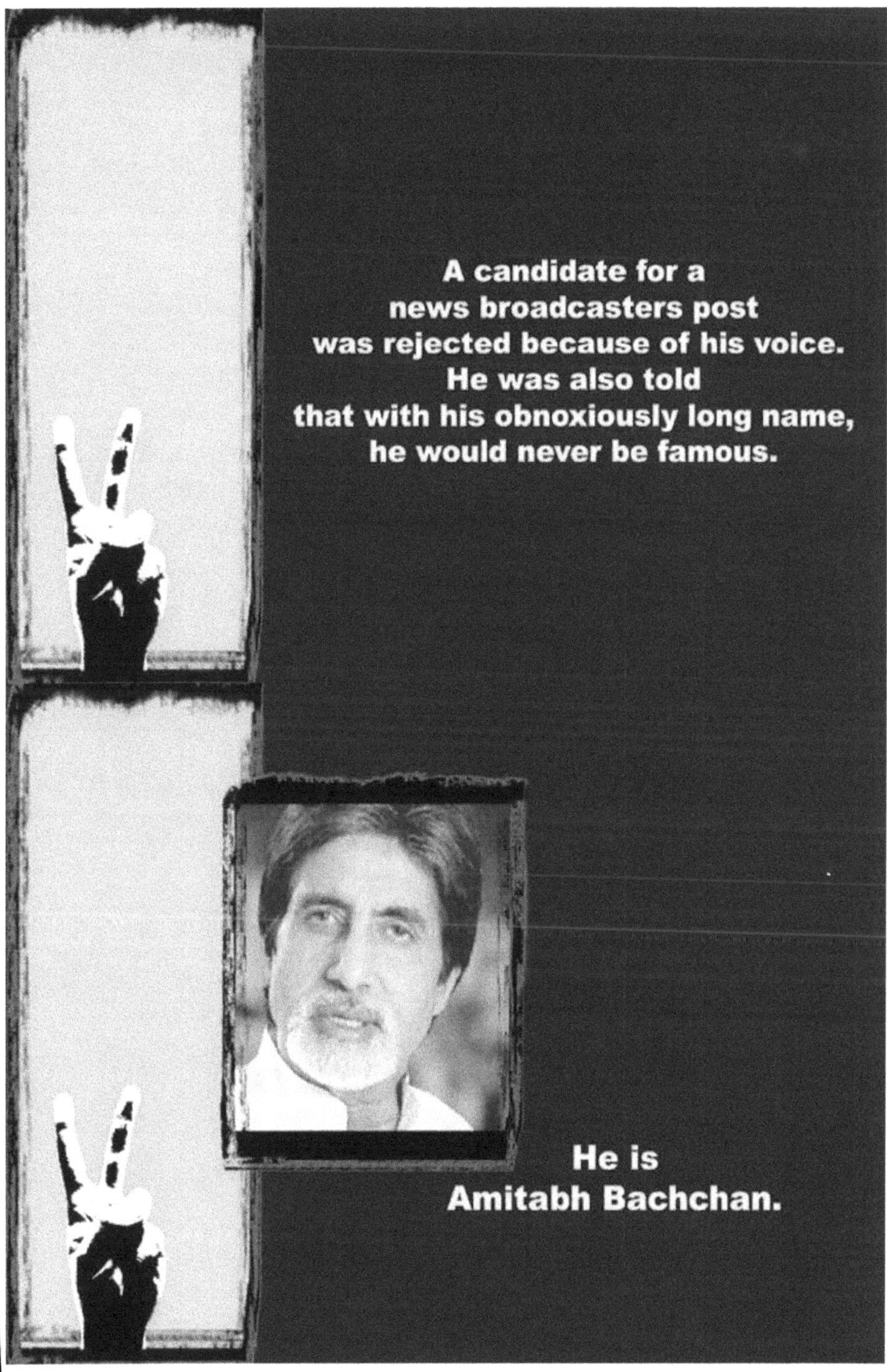

A candidate for a
news broadcasters post
was rejected because of his voice.
He was also told
that with his obnoxiously long name,
he would never be famous.

He is
Amitabh Bachchan.

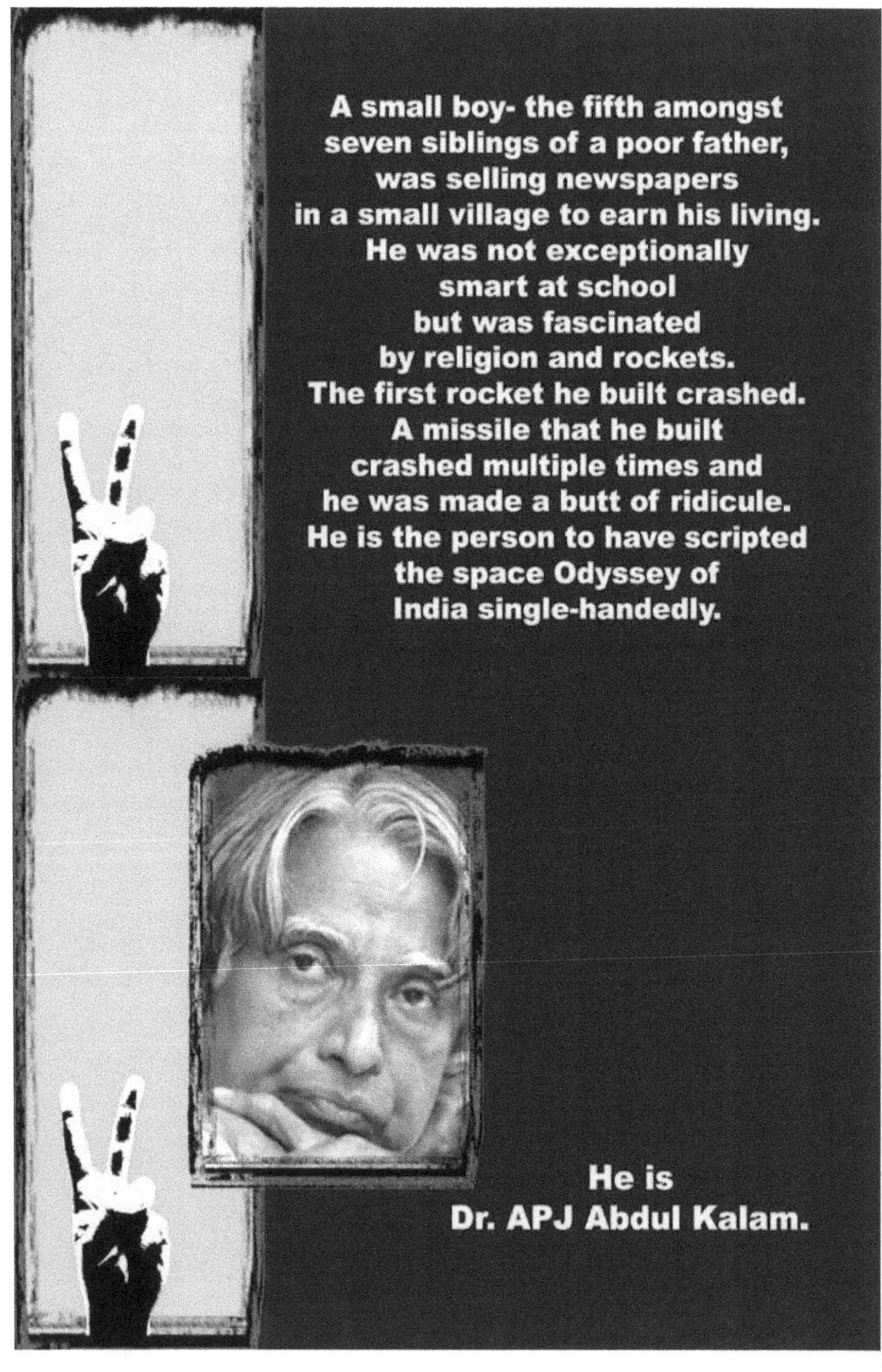
A small boy- the fifth amongst
seven siblings of a poor father,
was selling newspapers
in a small village to earn his living.
He was not exceptionally
smart at school
but was fascinated
by religion and rockets.
The first rocket he built crashed.
A missile that he built
crashed multiple times and
he was made a butt of ridicule.
He is the person to have scripted
the space Odyssey of
India single-handedly.
He is
Dr. APJ Abdul Kalam.

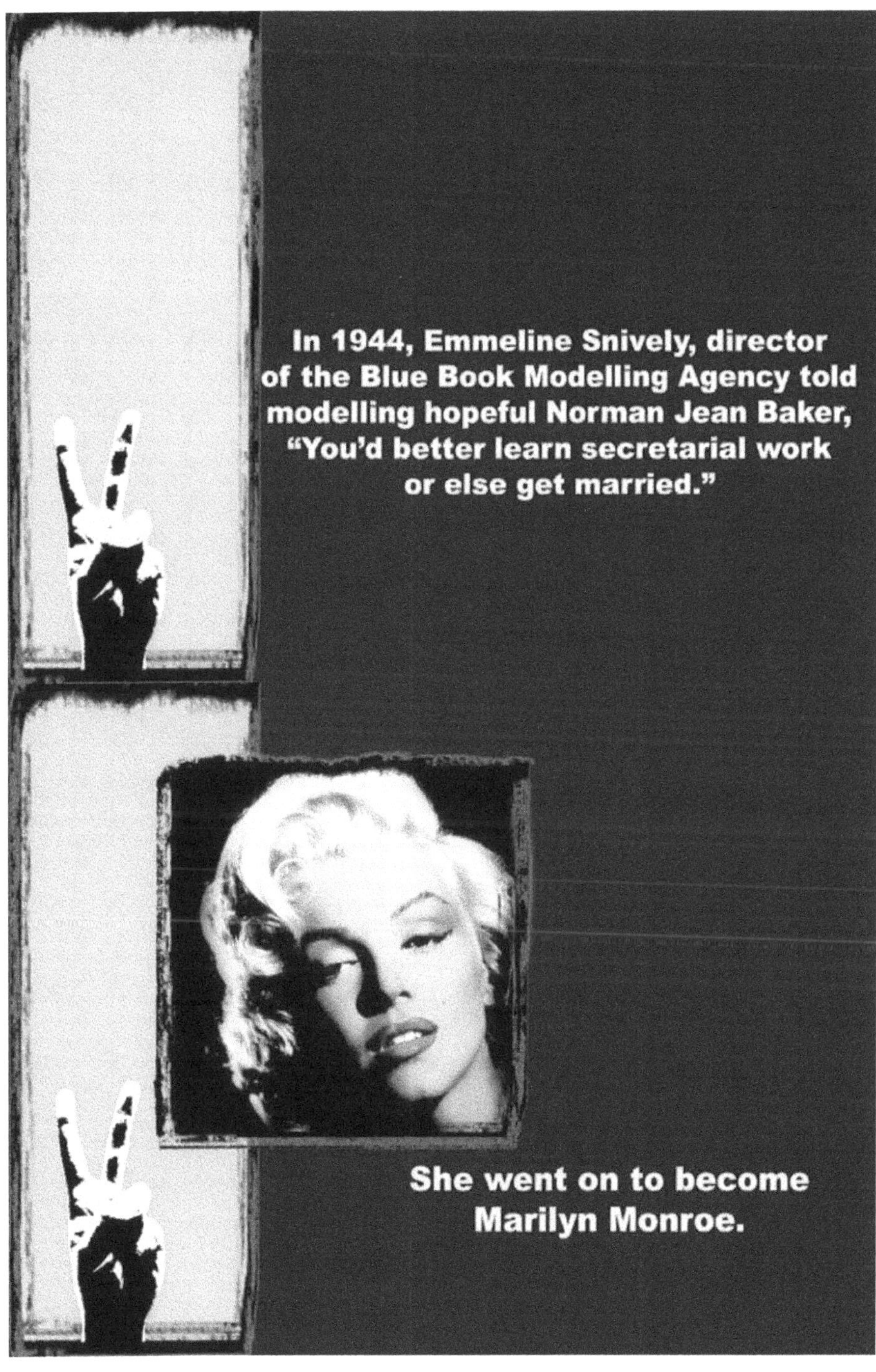

In 1944, Emmeline Snively, director
of the Blue Book Modelling Agency told
modelling hopeful Norman Jean Baker,
"You'd better learn secretarial work
or else get married."

She went on to become
Marilyn Monroe.

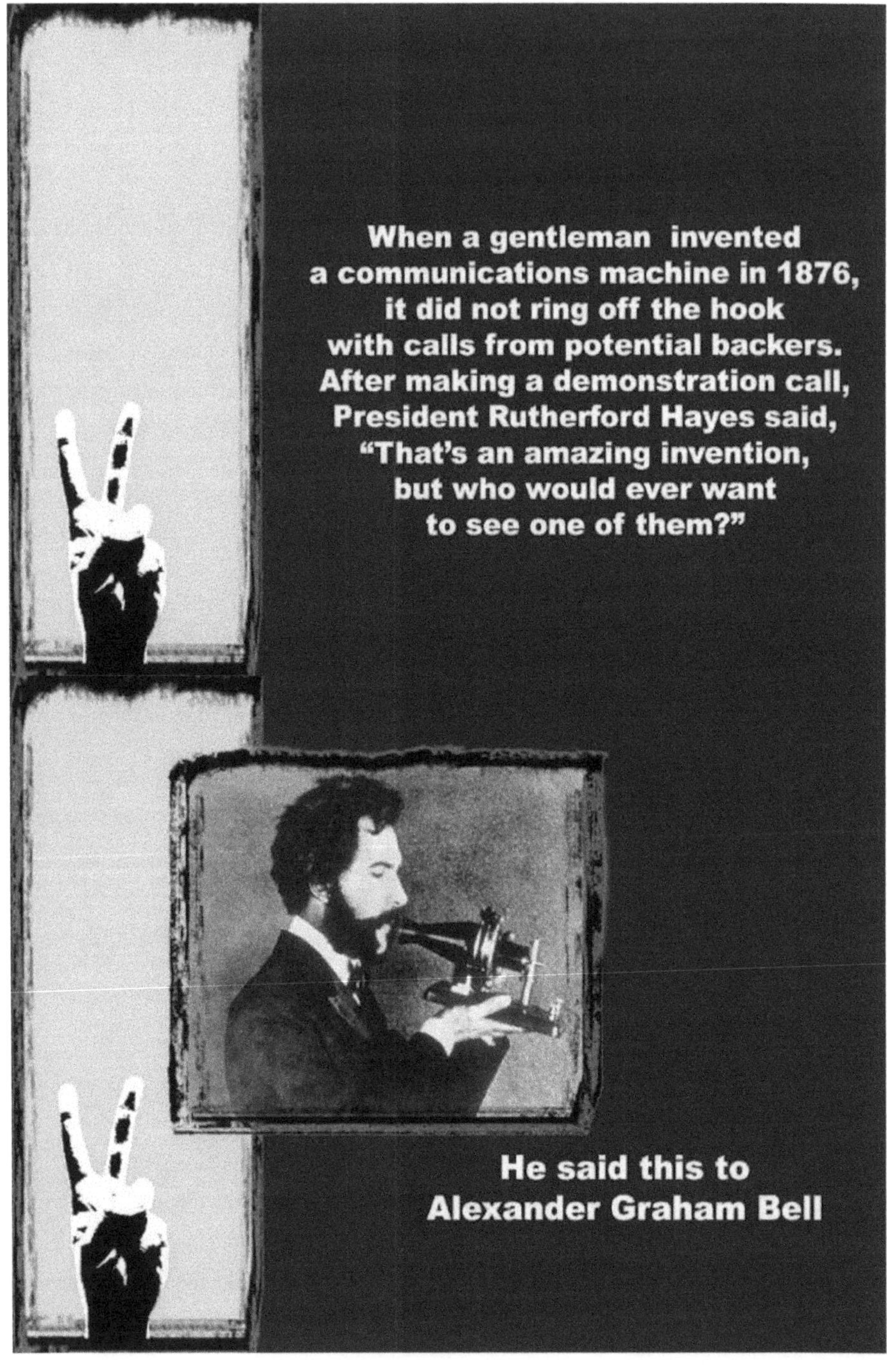

When a gentleman invented
a communications machine in 1876,
it did not ring off the hook
with calls from potential backers.
After making a demonstration call,
President Rutherford Hayes said,
"That's an amazing invention,
but who would ever want
to see one of them?"

He said this to
Alexander Graham Bell

In the 1940s another young inventor
named Chester Carlson took his idea
to 20 Corporations, including
some of the biggest in the country.
They all turned him down.
In 1947,
after seven long years of rejections!
He finally got a tiny company
in New York, the Haloid company,
to purchase the rights to his invention –
an electrostatic paper-copying process.
Haloid became Xerox Corporation.
Chester Carlson

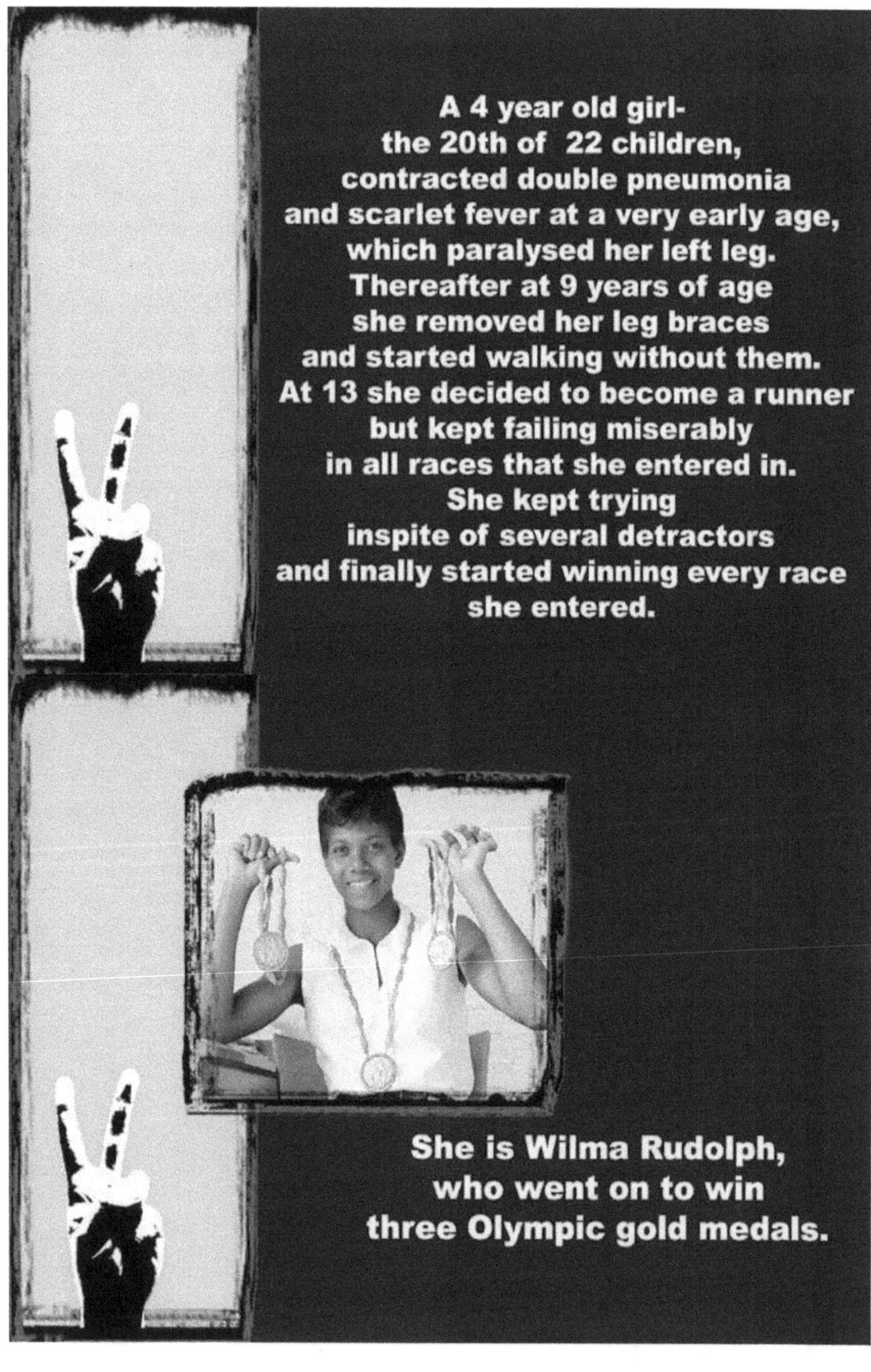

HOW TO BECOME A CELEBRITY LEADER IN HOSPITALITY INDUSTRY

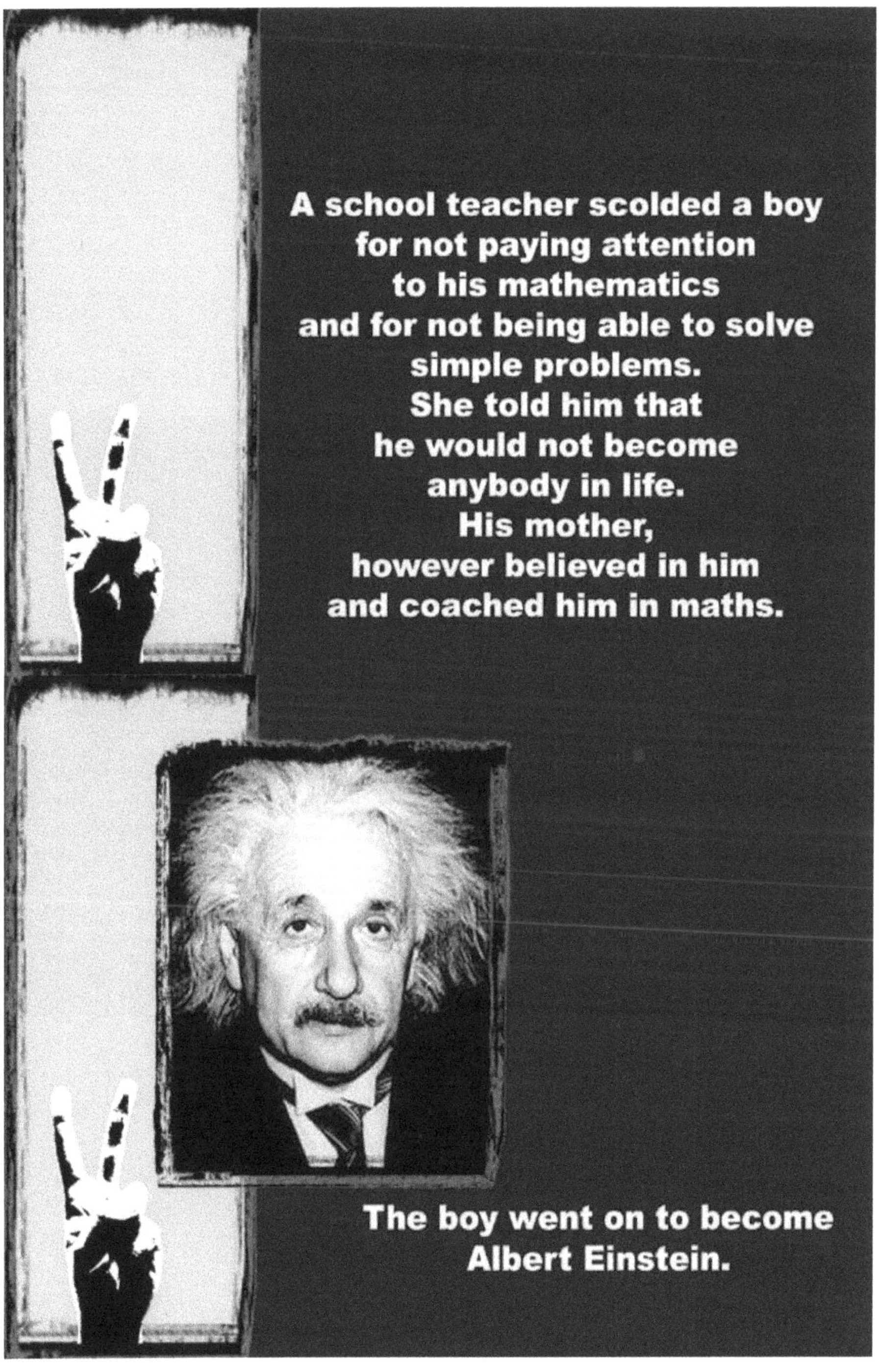

A school teacher scolded a boy
for not paying attention
to his mathematics
and for not being able to solve
simple problems.
She told him that
he would not become
anybody in life.
His mother,
however believed in him
and coached him in maths.
The boy went on to become
Albert Einstein.

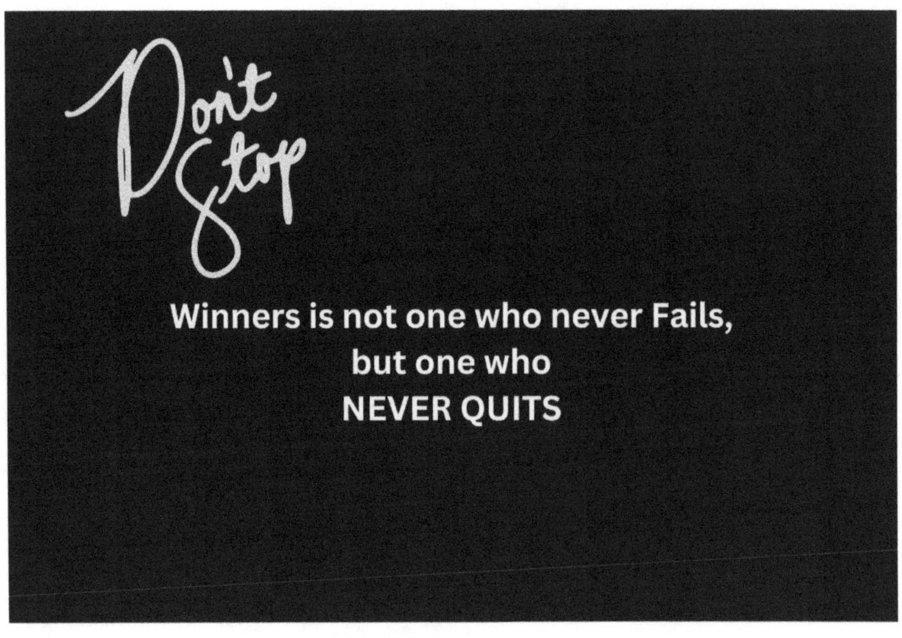

Don't Stop
Winners is not one who never Fails,
but one who
NEVER QUITS

20

The Winner's Edge vs. The Loser's Limitation

The winner is always part of the answer
The loser is always part of the problem

The winner always has a program
The loser always has an excuse

The winner says "Let me do it for you"
The loser says "That is not my job"

The winner sees an answer
for every problem
The loser sees a problem
for every answer

A winner makes commitments
A loser makes promises

When winner makes a mistake, he says, I was wrong
When loser makes a mistake, he says, it was not my fault

Winner has dream
Loser has scheme

Winner says "I must do something"

Loser says "something must be done"
Winner is part of the team
Loser is apart from the team

Winner always sees the gain
Loser always sees the pain

Winner is a thermostat
Loser is a thermometer

Winners use hard arguments
But soft words
Losers use soft arguments
But hard words

Winner makes it happen
Loser let it happen

I sincerely wish all of you become the winners & be a Celebrity Leader.

The content of this book has been explained into 2 parts

1. How a leader who wants to become a celebrity leader can make their root strong by focusing on 3 things

    A. Mind set

    B. Skill set

    C. Tool set

2. Once their root is strong then what good practices they should follow to win the hearts of their team members and make them die heart fans to get the work done very easily both qualitative and quantitative.

These good practices are described in details by applying 4C concepts.

C – Connection (Heart to Heart)
C – Communication (Positive & Clear)
C – Convert (them to fans)
C – Community. (Build a strong team).

During my 40 years stint in the Hospitality Industry I have guided many industry professionals using the above concepts and when they followed these principles meticulously, they become absolutely successful leaders and today they are commanding the Industry like kings.

So, I suggest to have piercing focus on Mind Set which will make your leadership root strong and no one will be able to knock down.

Then proceed to develop Skill Set & Tool Set.

Consistently follow the good practices by applying 4C concepts.

No one in this world can stop you from becoming a CELEBRITY LEADER.

GOOD LUCK